CALM DOWN

CALM DOWN

GARY COLLINS

CHRISTIAN HERALD BOOKS
Chappaqua, New York

We acknowledge with appreciation permission to quote from: *Today's Christian Woman* magazine and *Christian Herald* magazine, in which much of the material in this book originally appeared.

Library of Congress Cataloging in Publication Data

Collins, Gary R.
 Calm down.

1. Christian Life—1960- of life. I. Title	2. Conduct
BV4501.2.C643 248.4	81-65726
ISBN 0-915684-93-4 (pbk.)	AACR2

MEMBER OF
EVANGELICAL CHRISTIAN
PUBLISHERS ASSOCIATION

Christian Herald, independent, evangelical and interdenominational, is dedicated to publishing wholesome, inspirational and religious books for Christian families.

First Edition
CHRISTIAN HERALD BOOKS, 40 Overlook Drive, Chappaqua, New York 10514
Printed in the United States of America

Other Books by Gary R. Collins

Search for Reality
Living in Peace
Our Society in Turmoil (editor)
Man in Transition
Effective Counseling
Fractured Personalities
Man in Motion
Overcoming Anxiety
The Christian Psychology of Paul Tournier
Coping with Christmas
It's OK to Be Single (editor)
Make More of Your Marriage (editor)
The Secrets of Our Sexuality (editor)
Facing the Future (editor)
Living and Growing Together (editor)
How to Be a People Helper
People Helper Growthbook
The Rebuilding of Psychology: An Integration of
    Psychology and Christianity
You Can Profit from Stress
Family Talk
Helping People Grow (editor)
Christian Counseling: A comprehensive guide
Psychology and Theology

101283

CONTENTS

PREFACE:
how to handle
this book

I don't suppose it would be accurate to label me a "senior citizen"—especially now, while I'm still in my forties. At the place where I teach, however, I am a "senior faculty member," a tenured full professor who has been in one position for over a dozen years.

During that time I've taught a few basic courses over and over again to the different generations of students who shuffle dutifully through our halls of learning. As you can imagine, such repetition could get dull, so to prevent this we change the approach each time a course is taught. I try to update the material, change the illustrations, and even find new jokes in order to spare both professor and student from slow death by boredom. Then, a couple of times each year, I drop in a new course. It's always titled "Advanced Seminar," but it has different subject matter each time and is designed to add excitement and freshness to the curriculum—and to me!

Recently in the advanced seminar we took a long, hard look at self-help books like this one. We read articles and popular volumes on how to handle depression, marriage tension, problem kids, loneliness, divorce, pressure, singleness, parenthood, job failure, shyness, and a variety of other issues. We even found a self-help book telling us how to handle other self-help books! Then we read a pile of scholarly articles that analyzed the whole self-help movement in an effort to determine whether such books really do help.

They do!

Of course it isn't always easy to help yourself only by reading a book. Sometimes we also need to discuss our problems with a friend or counselor. At times we may read about problems, but nothing changes in our lives if we are unable or unwilling to apply what we read. Then there is the easy temptation to pull statements out of context and make them say something that the author never intended. That doesn't help anyone.

Nevertheless, most of us benefit from reading self-help books and applying what they suggest about the pressures of life. To live in this world is to experience stress, and at times all of us need help in calming down. To provide such help is the purpose of this volume.

Almost all the chapters in this book were published as magazine articles. They were not written for a book, but in view of the warm reception these articles received, I agreed to the publisher's request that the chapters be pulled together in more permanent form. We have tried to put them in a logical order, but each chapter stands alone and can be read in any order you wish.

You might even consider making them the basis of a church or neighborhood discussion group. You could read a chapter or two each week and then consider questions like these:

What did the chapter say that was helpful?

What does the chapter say that applies to you?

What does the Bible say about the subject discussed in this chapter?

In what ways could you change in the coming weeks as a result of reading and thinking about this chapter? Be specific.

How could the chapter help you to help others?

I sincerely hope this little volume will be used by God to help you and others to more effectively handle the pressures of life. If this happens—and I believe it can—I might even have my students discuss *this* book next time we have a seminar on self-help books. "Senior" professors like me can get away with scheduling courses like that. They're educational, helpful, and a lot of fun.

Happy reading!

Gary R. Collins

1

HOW TO HANDLE
pressure

Snow!

I like the memory of it, especially at the time of year when the weather is getting warmer and the long days of summer are coming upon us. It is pleasant to think back to the times in winter when freshly fallen snow would cover the streets with a blanket of whiteness, dust the evergreens with tufts of sparkling crystals, and fill the fields near our house with drifts that would reflect the blueness of a winter sky.

To be honest, I must admit that on wintry mornings these feelings aren't always uppermost in my mind, especially when the driveway needs to be shoveled, the wind is bitterly cold, the roads slippery, the traffic snarled. At such times the beauty of a winter storm is overshadowed by the pressures of trying to survive until spring.

One day last February we awoke to discover a howling blizzard swirling around our house. The radio announced that local schools were closed, and the kids, who had been dragging through breakfast, suddenly came alive and cheered the news of an unexpected holiday. I was less enthusiastic. The snow was influencing airport operations, and I wondered if it would be possible for me to leave as planned on a midafternoon flight to Iowa. That evening I was scheduled to give a talk on the subject of pressure.

Because of the storm, I left for the airport early, parked the car, checked my bag, and waited—not for one hour or two, but for eight. When the people in Iowa learned of my plight, they postponed the talk until the next day, while I vainly tried to find some way to get to Des Moines. All around me were frustrated people. Some were angry—very angry—and grumbled as if the United Airlines ticket agent had created the snow. Others were impatient, but many seemed to take the situation with good-natured humor. They cheered when the flight attendants appeared, and joked with one another. Inwardly, I was frustrated, but amused at the irony of the situation. Here I was, imprisoned in an airport and pressured by the realization that in another city two hundred people were waiting for me to give a talk on stress management. Unexpectedly, I had found myself with a whole day to ponder whether my conclusions about pressure really worked.

Pressure influences us in different ways, depending, it seems, on our attitudes, upbringing, past experiences, and personalities. Like my fellow travelers in the airport, some react to stress with anger, impatience, or humor. Some people worry, others get discouraged, and there are those who appear completely relaxed on the outside but who may be churning within. While some plunge into pessimism, others are buoyed by optimism. While many people do nothing, except to fret, others analyze the situation and logically decide what they can do, if anything, to reduce the pressure.

Regardless of our natural tendencies, there are several steps that can be taken to help us cope with the pressures of life.

Look to God. It is overwhelming to realize that God, who created the world and holds it all together, is also concerned about individual people and willing to help with our problems and pressures. The Bible tells us that God will guide, forgive, help, and teach believers as we journey through life. Jesus promised to give us inner peace, and we know that we are never ignored or forsaken by God (see, for example, Heb. 13:5–6; John 14:27).

This knowledge can sustain us, especially in times of

pressure. When difficulties arise, we can cast our anxieties on Him, in prayer, and know that God cares for us (I Pet. 5:7). Looking to God for help, wisdom, and guidance is always a first step in handling pressure.

Look at yourself. Most people, I suspect, realize that introspection can be overdone. A constant mulling over of our problems and woes can drag us into despair and inactivity. Often, however, there is value in looking inward and asking ourselves three questions.

First, ask what your body may be saying about the present pressures. In response to stress, the body automatically goes into a state of alert. Our heart beats faster, the blood composition changes, and the muscles tense—all in case we have to run, fight, or otherwise cope effectively with a crisis. Sometimes, inner physical changes warn us of a pressure build-up even before we are aware of it consciously. Headaches, muscle tension, shortness of breath, stomach upsets, and sinus problems are among the physical clues that tell us something is wrong.

As I waited for the plane on that blustery day last February, I became aware at one point that my stomach was upset. Tea and a little snack helped, but so did a walk to the ticket counter where I was able to discuss the situation briefly with a sympathetic but equally frustrated ticket agent.

As a second question, ask what you are feeling. Sometimes we seem to think that feelings are best squelched and put out of our mind. This rarely works. Denied feelings may be hidden from ourselves (and sometimes from others), but they are still inside, stirring us up and wearing us down.

Usually pressure is accompanied by feelings of anger, anxiety, discouragement, fear, and frustration. Sometimes there is a sense of futility, feelings of guilt, and an awareness of our own inadequacy. These feelings are best admitted and perhaps even shared with a friend. Then we can try to deal with the issues that are creating the pressure feelings in the first place.

Third, ask yourself what you are thinking. When we are

under pressure we sometimes don't think clearly. How easy it is to become complaining, negative, pessimistic, overly dependent on others, self-critical, and at times even irrational. These thoughts and mental attitudes can hinder effective problem solving and make the pressures worse. It is always wise, therefore, to pause even briefly to think about our mental attitudes. Is our thinking really logical and based on fact—or are we getting carried away with our worries and criticisms?

All this implies that we should make an effort to "take control of ourselves" in times of pressure. Taking a few minutes to relax physically, to admit our feelings and attitudes, to ponder the situation, and to decide calmly on a course of action—all this can be helpful in handling pressure.

Look at the environment. Have you ever noticed that some people and some places can be pressure-arousing? Let's look first at the people. Anxious, nervous individuals usually stimulate anxiety in others. Negative, critical people have a way of pulling others down. In times of pressure it is helpful to avoid such people whenever this is possible. In my airport wait, I pulled away from the crowded ticket counters and found a seat where I could read, away from the milling crowd.

There is value in trying to avoid stressful places. It is not easy to relax in a cluttered room or a noisy restaurant where dissonant music competes with the conversation of the dinner guests.

Of course retreat isn't always possible. Sometimes it is more important to stay with other pressured people who need our calming influence. But notice that even Jesus pulled away from the crowds and pressures of needy people. By Himself, in a lonely place, He prayed and apparently sensed the rejuvenation that enabled Him to carry on with His busy ministry (see Mark 1:32–39).

Look at the problem. Can you determine what precisely is causing your pressure? Is it, for example, a specific frustrating situation, an inner compulsion to accomplish something, the actions of another person, the influence of too much change, the lack of money or needed skills, the influence of the government or of one's employer, or the stress of too much work and too little time? This attempt to find a specific cause or causes of pressure is what one psychiatrist has called "focusing." When we can find the exact sources of pressure and focus our attention on these causes, we can do something about finding a solution to our problems.

Look for possible ways to reduce the pressure. When pressures build there is a tendency for us to blame others and assume that someone else is responsible for finding a solution to our problems. This is not a very effective way to handle pressure. It usually is better to:

• Decide if anything can be done, then do it. In my airport delay, I couldn't hasten the departure of my flight, but I did check for the availability of flights on other airlines, and I called ahead to let the people at my destination know that I was delayed.

• Try to reduce the number of tasks and the difficulty of what needs to be done. Can you get someone to help you? Can you decide which things just won't get done, and/or lower your perfectionist standards? Whenever we go on a trip my wife and I each have a list of things to be done before we leave. Almost never do we have time to finish everything. At some time before our departure we have to reduce our expectations and accept the fact that some things won't get done as well as we had hoped—if at all.

• Try to reduce the time pressure. Many of us are in a hurry—to succeed, to reach our goals, to finish our work projects. We are impatient people who don't like waiting. We value efficiency and live under a time pressure that intensifies stress and makes it more difficult for us to deal calmly with pressures when they do come. We must determine to slow down, to take more time, and to stop for periodic rest. By pacing ourselves we are more likely to live longer and go through life with a lot less pressure.

● Try to reduce the number of changes in life. Sometimes the biggest source of pressure is from ourselves. By scheduling too many activities, we find ourselves running all the time and barely able to keep up with a frantic pace which is of our own creation. When there are too many activities and changes in life, it is easy to panic but difficult to cope. Insofar as we can, we should learn to eliminate some of the change and alter the hectic lifestyle.

Look to the future. It is wiser and healthier to avoid pressure before it comes, rather than trying to deal with its consequences once the pressure arrives. By examining the way we live, pondering how we can slow down as part of our life style, and thinking now about coming pressures, we can learn to cope more effectively. As with disease, so with pressure— an ounce of prevention is worth a pound of cure.

When I finally got out of that airport last winter and went to give my speech on pressure, I felt good. The principles outlined in these paragraphs had worked, and it was fun sharing them with the audience.

But then, somebody presented me with an important challenge. "Be careful," my friend began, "that you don't try to get rid of pressure altogether. A tire without pressure doesn't do its job—and neither do people." This is true, of course. Some pressure can be good. It motivates us and keeps us alert. But too much pressure can immobilize and bring us to the point of explosion. When we can learn to handle it effectively, it can help rather than hinder our activities.

This is true in the summer, as well as during snowstorms.

2

HOW TO HANDLE
boredom

It must have been spectacular, that night when Bennetto School burned to the ground. It was a drafty old building with long corridors and high beams which ignited like tinder, sending brilliant orange flames up through the roof into the midnight sky. Watching from the crowd, there surely were kids who cheered, at least silently, but some of the parents and older people must have grieved inside as our rambling old grammar school ended its life in a blaze of glory.

I learned a lot during my days in Bennetto School. In the early grades they taught us how to read and write. There we were introduced to history, geography, English, music, art, and math. Away from our mothers during the day, we learned to get along with other kids and with the teachers. Some were warm and encouraging; others were like my fourth-grade teacher, so irritable and crabby that they made a misery out of education.

Most of the time it also was boring. Like generations before me, I at times wrote *"bored* of education" in the pages of my notebooks or scratched it on the desk tops, along with my initials. At the time I would have agreed with the teenager who later complained that schools are training grounds for boredom—places that prepare people for tedious nine-to-five jobs.

In my old school I learned to daydream and to tuck more

interesting reading material behind the textbooks we were told to study. This early experience started me on a lifetime search for ingenious ways to occupy my mind whenever I am bored. Now the problem is most acute in faculty meetings, church business sessions, and whenever I am in front of a television set. At such times, an inconspicuous book can do wonders to prevent death by boredom.

Before my old school burned down, I used to sit in class and think that boredom would end as soon as I graduated. That, of course, didn't happen. Boredom, I soon discovered, is an inescapable part of life. "If the 1950s were the age of anxiety," writes psychologist Sam Keen, then "the 1970s and 80s are the Age of Melancholy and Boredom." Psychoanalyst Erich Fromm called boredom the "illness of the age" in which we live. It hits people in all vocations, both young and old, and while it has been around for decades, its power may be especially great in the late twentieth century. Surrounded by labor-saving devices and almost limitless opportunities for stimulation, thousands of us still are bored with school, housework, retirement, church, marriage, or unfulfilling jobs. Even leisure activities can be boring; movies, sports, cocktail or coffee parties, traveling, hobbies can each grow stale. If you don't agree, ask any person who is retired or out of work.

Adding to the problem is our tendency in North America to deny that we are bored. For some reason, many of us see boredom as a sign of weakness and an indication that we aren't creative enough to amuse ourselves in this society of "go-getters." As a result, we scramble to find "meaningful" things to do, we eat or sleep too much in an unconscious attempt to fill the void, we fill up our time with various forms of entertainment, and when all else fails we slip into one or both of the two most common but destructive reactions to boredom: drug use and violence. According to Dr. Fromm, boredom is the major source of aggression in twentieth-century America. Philosopher Bertrand Russell would have agreed. "Boredom is a vital problem," he wrote. "At least half the sins of mankind are caused by the fear of it."

These conclusions may be interesting and disturbing, but how do they apply to us? How do we handle boredom in our own lives? Let's consider three practical issues.

What is boredom? Boredom is a feeling of emptiness and monotony that comes when we have nothing to do. To be bored is to feel blasé, apathetic, unenthusiastic about everything, tired of sameness, and frustrated because time passes so slowly. When we're bored, it is difficult to make decisions, and often we have a "what's the use" attitude. We long for stimulation, but if the boredom persists we feel tired, discouraged, and often angry.

Most psychology students have heard about the famous "sensory deprivation" experiments which were done several years ago in Canada. Student volunteers were blindfolded and asked to lie on a bed in a soundproof room. While there was time out for meals (which they ate sitting on the edge of the bed) and for going to the toilet, the students spent the rest of their time alone with their hands covered by gloves and cardboard cuffs to prevent them from feeling anything.

At first the students in this experiment slept, and then they daydreamed—planning work, thinking about leisure activities, or even playing mental games. After several hours, however, these people were confronted with intense boredom. They got irritable, apathetic, confused, and frustrated. "I couldn't think of anything to think about," one reported later, and after several days some students even began to experience hallucinations.

Boredom is like this in real life. For a while we can handle it, especially if we know it is temporary. When it persists, however, our bordom can be painful and disruptive. While hoping for change and excitement, we instead feel uninspired, disappointed, and not inclined to do much of anything. Often we find our creativity squelched and our resentment building, especially when we are in the presence of anyone who shows enthusiasm and happiness. Like the students in that Canadian experiment, we find ourselves slipping into irritability, apathy, confusion, and frustration.

Unlike some other common problems, however, there is a way out of boredom. The first step is to understand its causes.

What causes boredom? Boredom comes either because we are in a monotonous environment, or because we have developed a frame of mind which leads us to conclude that a situation is boring.

Some things *are* boring, and this should be recognized. Routine work on an assembly line can be monotonous and so are the lives of some housewives, traveling salesmen, and even pastors. Many people find it boring to be alone or to work in jobs that never seem to be done. Some interesting World War II studies showed that efficiency drops quickly and boredom blossoms whenever people must spend long periods of time doing the same thing, like standing watch in a military situation. Most of us could agree with Christopher Burney, a British secret agent who was imprisoned in solitary confinement by the Nazis. After his release, Burney wrote that "variety is not the spice of life; it is the very stuff of life."

Sometimes, however, too much variety can also be boring. An endless barrage of vocational challenges, excessive competition, television input, or family demands can give us plenty of stimulation, but we are left feeling bored and exhausted from running too long with a full-steam-ahead mentality. Sometimes when Christians get caught up in a busy ministry or with the pressure to be always enthusiastic and joyful, there is boredom, fatigue, and a longing to experience the rejuvenation that comes from a more balanced, relaxed life style.

Our life styles, like our perspectives on boredom, often depend on how we look at the world. Don't you know people who work in boring jobs, but who try to see the value in what they are doing and who refuse to dwell on the fact that their work is repetitious? In contrast, most of us have read about influential political people or artists and sports celebrities whose lives are filled with excitement, acclaim, and glit-

ter, but who are bored by it all and who complain—
sometimes in radio interviews or in newspaper articles—that
life is monotonous. A lot depends on our attitude.

What, then, can we do about boredom? First, take courage in
the fact that boredom is common. Most people get bored, at
least periodically, but this could be a friend in disguise—a
challenge which motivates us to make some changes so that
life will be more satisfying and productive.

Second, resist the temptation to jump into a variety of
new activities. Afraid of boredom and sometimes threatened
by its presence, our Western mentality urges us to get busy in
an attempt to defeat the problem. Changing jobs (or mates),
finding a new hobby, going on a trip, rushing to cultural and
sports events, enrolling in seminars or college courses—all
these can bring stimulation and perhaps temporary relief, but
such activity can also create pressure, exhaustion, and more
boredom.

More effective than busy activity is a third suggestion:
take some time to evaluate your life. Why are you bored? Are
you too pressured, unable to see any purpose in your life,
unwilling to strike a balance between your work-family-
church-relaxation and other responsibilities? Is your attitude
a part of the problem? Have you outgrown your job?

Recently I met a man who shared his opinion about
writers. "It must be wonderful," he stated, "to sit at a type-
writer and experience the excitement of words tumbling from
your creative mind and onto the paper." Perhaps this is an
accurate description of some authors, but it doesn't describe
me or the writers I know. Most of us have to push ourselves
to keep going. We struggle against the temptation to be
distracted by other things. Long hours of research and reading sometimes produce very little creative writing and, to be
honest, the work can be exhausting and boring.

But the work can also stretch writers, free them to be
creative, and lead to books or articles that can be informative
and helpful. Whenever I get bored, therefore, I try to evaluate
why. I try to see my work and life in terms of their overall

purpose and influence. I admit to myself that tedium is sometimes necessary if we are to be creative and fulfilled. "A life too full of excitement is an exhausting life," a wise philosopher once wrote. "A generation that cannot endure boredom will be a generation of little people." For all of us, there must be times for reflection and rejuvenation.

A fourth approach to boredom is to ponder the dangers of taking risks. In thinking about the boredom that so often comes in mid-life, I recently read a book about some people who changed careers after ten-fifteen years in their chosen vocations. Most had begun their adult lives with hope and enthusiasm, but soon disillusionment, anger, and feelings of powerlessness had led to depression and boredom. These men wanted to change careers, but the risk of abandoning their security and trying something new was almost overwhelming. Then they realized that the alternative to risk-taking is perpetual boredom.

Certainly we can act irresponsibly and without careful planning. Who, for example, can know how many people have changed jobs or marriages in an ill-considered attempt to escape boredom, and then spent the rest of life living with regret? Nevertheless, it can be helpful to evaluate our life situation with its values, feelings, and frustrations. Should we stay where we are or take the risk of trying something new?

If we believe in divine guidance, we can seek God's direction daily and use our God-given brains to make decisions about the future. Like the apostle Paul, we sometimes will decide to remain in one place for a while, but at other times we may find ourselves moving, changing jobs, altering our attitudes, or risking involvement in some new venture. As pilgrims on earth, we need a willingness to make periodic changes and to take risks. This willingness, followed by occasional risky action, is a strong cure for boredom.

Fifth, we must rethink the role of fantasy in our lives. It seems that evangelical Christians—especially those who are well educated—resist any suggestion that we should let our minds wander, ponder dreams, or dwell on creative possibilities for the future. It is true, of course, that daydreaming can put us out of touch with reality. Escape into a fantasy world of novels, unrealistic wishing, or sinful lust can so captivate the mind that our actual world seems dull or boring in comparison. Nevertheless, when imagination stimulates us to plan creatively and to think about possibilities for change, then such fantasy can be a great antidote to boredom.

Sixth, it would seem wise to resist the temptation to withdraw into frequent TV viewing. Might it be that television is a major cause of our modern boredom? Encouraged to be passive, dependent on others for excitement; molded by the values and opinions of television writers or commentators; and discouraged from thinking or communicating with live human beings, we could become a nation of passive, manipulated zombies. Dr. Sam Keen has argued that commercial television mesmerizes viewers so that we no longer ask questions, but respond unconsciously to the messages of advertisers who "sell us dreams of a gadget-filled utopia." Television may create boredom, rather than dispelling it.

Finally, there is value in reaching out. Sometimes, it seems, we are so caught up in concern about ourselves that we have forgotten others. But what could be more boring than a me-centered life which has no intimacy, no commitment to others, and no compassion? Jesus took time to be alone and with God, but He also showed love and concern to those with whom He came into contact. The Bible never leaves the impression that our Lord had a problem with boredom.

I wish I had learned some of this during my student days at Bennetto School, before that stately old structure collapsed in flames. Boredom can be painful, but it also can stimulate us to reexamine our lives, our work, our fantasies, our willingness to take risks, and our involvement with others. Perhaps being "bored" with education wasn't so bad after all.

3

HOW TO HANDLE
habits

Victor Borge has a delightful little routine about coughing.

Before playing one of his musical selections on the piano, he tells the audience that anyone who feels the need to cough should do so before the music begins.

Then he pauses!

Within seconds, somebody coughs, and before long the whole concert hall is filled with coughing (and laughing) people. The mere suggestion of a cough gets people started.

I thought of this recently when I was doing some work in a local public library. A rather rotund lady (that's putting it graciously) came into the room and positioned herself at a table near mine.

Almost immediately she started coughing! It wasn't the deep and hearty kind of cough that comes with a cold or bronchitis. It was more a throat-clearing kind of noise that was both distracting and addictive. Within five minutes I found myself coughing as well, even though I was trying valiantly not do so so. Like Victor Borge's audiences, I had been taken over by the subtle power of suggestion. Since it was time for a coffee break, I left the library temporarily, and when I returned (without my cough) the lady and her throat tickle were gone.

Constant coughing can become a habit—like nail biting, yelling, masturbating, smoking, or even nodding our heads in unique ways. We all have such habits. We learn them early in life, and later they are seen in the way we think, talk, walk, and sit. Next time you go to church watch the preacher's gestures, facial expressions, mannerisms, and way of standing in the pulpit. Better still, watch the people in your family. Like you, they have habitual ways of acting and reacting. We may not like some of our habits, but most of them will get more and more ingrained as we get older and "set in our ways."

Consider, for example, one of the most common and frustrating habits in our culture: overeating. There is a host of reasons for this, including medical disorders with a physical basis. More often, however, overeating appears to be a learned habit that is extremely difficult to control. According to the director of a government-financed obesity research center at St. Luke's Hospital in New York City, our culture teaches us to eat more than we need. In the United States and Canada, "nutritious, palatable, calorically rich foods" are available to almost everyone, and they are advertised in alluring, tempting ways. People are encouraged to eat at parties, at movies, while watching TV, at work, and even during the fellowship hours in church. The prevalence of labor-saving devices, our dependence on cars, and the absence of sidewalks, all discourage exercise, encourage a sedentary life, and bring on obesity. Eating too much and exercising too little become bad habits which many of us try to break with the help of reducing pills, diet books, and weight-loss programs. In a recent year, Americans spent over $16,000 every minute ($8 billion a year) on diet aids. Perhaps millions of tons were shed, but according to one researcher, for every ten pounds lost through diets, the average person gains ten and one-half pounds back.

What can we do about overeating and other habits that we want to change? There are no fast, easy, "always-work" answers, but several approaches are worth considering. Each has worked with some people. When two or more are combined, the success rate is even better.

The willpower approach. Probably all of us have tried this at times. We do something that we don't want to do. Then we feel so guilty, discouraged, or angry with ourselves that we determine to stop forever. Sometimes we even pray about this and promise God that we will "never do it again." We may take pride in our new self-control, but before long we fail again and the cycle repeats itself. After a while we give up and sometimes find excuses for not changing. We become somewhat like the two-hundred-pound, fifteen-year-old girl who went to a weight clinic for five months and lost less than one pound. She didn't like overeating, but since it was more fun to eat then to diet, she gave up and told her doctor that she'd try again, but later.

Relying on willpower is perhaps the most often-tried and least-successful of all approaches to changing habits. Sometimes this method works; most often it does not.

In a way, however, willpower is basic to whatever else we may attempt. If we really don't want to change, we won't be motivated to try. If we don't try, we will be defeated before we begin. But such a discouraging attitude isn't necessary.

If you've tried and failed repeatedly, it is worth trying again. As you do so, try to resist the two common attitudes that are the downfall of many people.

First, there is the belief that "I'm the only one." That probably isn't true! Everybody has habits that they'd like to change, and it is likely that many people have struggles almost identical to yours.

Second, there is the conclusion that "I'll never change." That can also be wrong, especially if your troublesome habit is also a sinful habit. God doesn't want us to be slaves to self-defeating compulsions. He can guide us to freedom.

The environment approach. One way to handle habit-forming temptations is to remove yourself from the places and things that cause you to fall. The man with a temptation to drink shouldn't have lunch in bars. The woman who is trying to break a smoking habit should sit in the nonsmoking section of the restaurant. The person who habitually dwells on lustful thoughts must destroy any pornographic materials in his possession.

Destroying the source of temptation is only a temporary measure, of course. It is impossible to avoid temptation completely, and the problem habit ultimately must be attacked at some deeper level.

The psychological approaches. As we all know, troublesome habits are ingrained, automatic, and often pleasurable. Some habits, like too much eating, are even encouraged by society. (Have you ever gone on a diet, only to hear well-meaning friends and waitresses say that you, of all people, really aren't overweight, even though you look and feel like a blimp?) Change sometimes is very slow, and the results are so long in coming that we stop trying.

In order to overcome these habits, some psychologists have suggested a relearning approach. These experts argue that if habits are learned, they can be unlearned and replaced with something more desirable. Such unlearning is often most effective when guided by a counselor-teacher, but there are some things we can do ourselves. We can set some realistic, specific goals, monitor our behavior carefully, and reward ourselves when we do well.

As a student, I used this approach to cope with my habit of procrastination. I would decide, for example, to read a certain number of pages during an evening (that was the specific goal). I'd keep a record of pages read each day (that was self-monitoring mixed with self-competition), and when I reached the daily goal, I'd reward myself with time off, a nap, or something else that I wanted. The joys of graduation were too far away to have any meaningful effect on my day-to-day behavior, but these other gimmicks kept me going as a student. Even now I count calories, recording my daily totals in a book, and often I keep a little graph of time spent in private devotional time with God. These techniques help me with my habits of eating too much and procrastinating at spiritual exercises.

Another psychological approach is to replace one habit with another. If someone has a problem with habitual lust, deciding not to lust isn't going to help much, especially if there are pornographic materials hidden in the house where they can be viewed during a time of weakness. The temptations must be removed, and there must be an effort to fill the mind with nonlustful thoughts. Some people, for example, quote Scripture to themselves when they are tempted to dwell on harmful and resistance-weakening mental images.

The same is true of bitterness. For some people, bitter, angry, critical thinking has become habitual, and this can create all kinds of problems for oneself and others (Heb. 12:15). The solution is to let our minds be filled with thoughts of what is true, good, right, pure, lovely, and pleasing to God (Phil. 4:8).

Sometimes, of course, replacing one habit with another doesn't help much. Some smokers discover that they replace cigarettes with excessive food or nail biting. In such cases, one harmful habit has been replaced by another, and it may be wise to ask why this is so.

Another psychological approach to habit change is searching for causes. Many habits come from nothing more complicated than a tendency to do what our parents taught. We overeat because everybody did this at home. Unconsciously we pick up some mannerism or figure of speech because it is an obvious characteristic in someone whom we admire and want to emulate.

Perhaps you've heard about the little girl who asked why her mother always folded back the ends of the dough before putting the bread loaf into the oven. The mother replied that she did it because it was always done by her mother. Three generations then approached the great-grandmother and discovered that in her prime the baking pans were so short that the dough had to be folded to fit. A habit, originating because of a need, had been passed on and maintained because of the example shown by several generations of mothers.

There are times when habits are symptoms of some underlying problems or insecurities. Nail-biting, for example, is widely viewed as a tension-reducing habit. Some research has even shown that nail-biters, as a group, are more anxious then nonbiters. Overeating sometimes hides inner depression, worry, anger, boredom, insecurity, or a fear of relating to people. Masturbation, while common in adolescents, may persist in adults who are lonely, sexually maladjusted, or afraid of intimacy and the opposite sex.

If a habit resists all efforts to change, it might be helpful to ponder your inner problems. By yourself, or with the help of a friend or counselor, list your private struggles and consider some ways in which these can be resolved. By alleviating stress and learning to handle life more effectively, harmful habits sometimes take care of themselves.

It also is helpful to enlist the aid of another person. Even that coughing lady in the library could be more sensitive to this habit and better able to change if her husband or some other person could remind her whenever she cleared her throat. Some recent weight-loss research at Stanford demonstrated the importance of a mate's support when one is on a diet. When the husband or wife offers encouragement, interest in regular weigh-ins, praise for progress, and helpful suggestions, the dieting person loses more than those who diet without the spouse's encouragement.

I'm a great believer in accountability. It's easier to change if you can find a friend who will pray with you and for you, be available to offer support or encouragement when you feel weak, and check with you at regular times to get a report on how you are doing. Alcoholics Anonymous discovered this many years ago, and so have generations of persons with other undesirable habits. If you are dieting, for example, you can *always* find some private excuse to cheat, but the knowledge that you will have to give a report to a friend next week can be a powerful deterrent to both excuse-making and giving in to the habit.

The spiritual approach. In his recent book *How to Say No to a Stubborn Habit*, Erwin Lutzer has observed that "the chains of habit are so light you cannot feel them, until they are so strong you cannot break them." At such times it is only God who can give us freedom and help us change.

We must start by admitting to God that a habit has us beaten. Ask Him both to help you change and to believe that change is possible. If your habit involves sin, confess this and thank God that without question He forgives sin when we ask Him to do so (I John 1:9).

No psychology book will tell you this, but the Bible clearly states that Satan is alive and active in the world. He is a master of mental manipulation, and he will attempt to convince you that your habit is unchangeable.

Nonsense!

Christ's death and resurrection has defeated the devil, although he currently has some temporary freedom to cause havoc in the universe, and in you. When we "submit to Christ," however, we can consciously resist the devil and know that he will flee (James 4:7).

I once heard a pastor state that whenever he felt temptation he would say something like this: "Satan, in the name of Jesus Christ I command you to leave. The blood of Jesus Christ cleanses me from all sin." While I hesitate to propose something that might look like a magical formula, this *is* biblical (I John 1:7); it is consistent with the command to overtly resist the devil when he brings sinful habits into our lives.

Ultimately we must admit that we are responsible for our own behavior and habits. God didn't creat us with robot minds, programmed to do whatever He wanted and without any human freedom. In spite of Freud's view that we are helpless victims of our unconscious and childhood past, ultimately it is you and I who decide whether to eat excessively, to remove ourselves from tempting situations, to work at learning new habits, to fill our minds with healthy images, to seek the help of others, or to try to uncover and deal with underlying, habit-forming problems. If we decide to change, God will help and supply the strength we need.

It won't be easy, but if habits really are learned, then they can be unlearned, even when the habit is nothing more than coughing in the DuPage County Library.

4

HOW TO HANDLE
depression

When I emerged from graduate school, clutching my diploma and eager to change the world, I told God that I was ready to go wherever he directed—providing it was to a warm climate. God's ways are not always our ways, of course, and soon I found myself teaching at a liberal arts college in Minnesota. The people there were warm, but the weather definitely was not, especially in mid-February.

Every winter, it seemed, I would feel "down" as the cold, the ice, and the dreary days persisted with their relentless discomfort and inconvenience. Later I discovered that this midwinter discouragement is a common reaction among those of us who live in the north. It even has been given a name: cabin fever, which means feeling depressed, tired, and housebound, as the winter drags on and the warm brightness of spring seems to be nowhere in sight. Usually, however, the depression that comes with cabin fever disappears as the days get longer, the flowers burst into blossom, and the snows melt into the ground.

It would be encouraging if all depression would drift away like morning mists dissipate whenever the warm sun rises. But depression is not handled that easily. Neither is it limited to northern climates, caused only by dreary winters, nor limited to a few people with cabin fever.

Depression is one of the most common and most complicated of human emotional conditions. It affects people of all ages and positions in life, under all living conditions. Although depression tends to be more common in women than in men, it victimizes both sexes and creates indescribable misery. It affects some people more severely than others, can persist for a long or a short period of time, and comes somewhat without warning or apparent reason. So common is the experience, at least in its milder forms, that in the opinion of some psychologists people who claim to be depression-free probably are just unable to recognize the symptoms.

What is depression? Depression is a mild or intense experience of sadness, pessimism, self-condemnation, and apathy. It often involves overwhelming feelings of unworthiness, frustration, or despair. At times it is accompanied by insom-

---

DEPRESSION CHECKLIST

Please check each of the following experiences that you have had during the past week.

_____ Feeling unhappy, sad, and "blue"
_____ Loss of interest or pleasure in normal activities
_____ Feelings of inefficiency
_____ Feeling worthless and self-critical
_____ Loss of appetite
_____ Sleep difficulties (including insomnia and too much sleep)
_____ Low energy and feelings of exhaustion
_____ Restlessness and impatience
_____ Feeling guilty
_____ Hopeless feelings
_____ Trouble concentrating and making decisions
_____ Increased tendency to criticize
_____ Thoughts of death or suicide

nia, loss of appetite, guilt, anger, restlessness, an inability to "get going" and, in some cases, thoughts of suicide. The "Depression Checklist" summarizes the major symptoms of this common but disturbing condition.

What causes depression? This is a difficult question to answer. Depression is often triggered by the stresses of life—financial reversals, failure, family problems, physical illness, boredom, or even the persistence of a long, dreary winter.

Often depression-producing stresses result from losses, including the loss of people. Death, divorce, or prolonged separation can create depression. One can lose an opportunity, job promotion, status, self-respect, health, freedom, or hope. During a recent gasoline shortage, the story was told of an elderly man who took his own life because his work of delivering newspapers by car required more gasoline than he could get. The loss of fuel, and hence of his livelihood, created more depression than he could handle.

In addition to the experience of a loss, the psychiatry books list other causes which alone or together can lead to depression.

• Depression, for example, may arise from rejection. When parents ignore their children, deprive them of love, reject them, or set unrealistic goals (so that failure is probable), depression is more likely in childhood and/or in later life. Similar rejection by a spouse, children, or others can also cause depression.

• Depression may arise from feelings of helplessness. It is easy to get depressed if we feel that success never comes regardless of how hard we try, or if we live in a situation that seems hopeless and unchangeable. At such times we are inclined to give up, to develop a pessimistic perspective, and to slide into self-pity and a sense of hopelessness.

• Depression may arise from hurt and anger. This is one of the most widely accepted causes for depression. First we are hurt in some way. This arouses our anger and the desire for revenge. But many of us don't recognize or like to admit our hostile feelings, so we keep them hidden inside. This, in turn, wears us down and leads to depression.

• Depression may arise from sin and guilt. Guilt and depression go together so often that it is difficult to determine which came first. At times we feel guilty because of what we have done or failed to do. At other times guilt comes because we have failed to meet our own expectations or those of someone else. This is a special problem for Christians. Taught that we should always be victorious, joyful, and free of anger or discouragement, it is easy to feel guilty and condemn ourselves when we fail to meet such high standards.

• Depression may arise from low self-esteem. This has been implied in the preceding paragraphs. Periodically most of us struggle with feelings of inferiority, but during times of depression there often is an intense conviction that we are inept, inadequate, and incompetent. When we become convinced of our own inferiorities it is easy to get discouraged.

• Depression may arise from physical influences. Poor eating or sleeping habits, insufficient exercise, physical illnesses, brain tumors, biochemical disturbances, genetic factors—all these can influence the body and subsequently affect our emotions.

Depression clearly has no one cause, and neither does it have a simple cure. In their enthusiasm to be helpful some writers and popular speakers have implied that depression can be stopped simply by an act of will. But complete problems rarely have such simple solutions.

What, then, can be done about depression? First, recognize it. In our desire for fulfilled Christian living, we often fear depression and assume that it is a mark of incompetence and spiritual failure. It gives us little comfort to know that David, Elijah, Job, and a number of other biblical people—including Jesus (Matt. 26:37–38)—appear to have been depressed at some time in life. But psychologist Roger Barrett argues: "We need to see that there can be no mountain peaks if there are no valleys. There can be no victories if there are no struggles.

Think of the irrational and illogical nature of promising a constantly victorious existence that would not involve struggles. What would you then have victory over?"

When you are depressed, perhaps having checked several of the items on the depression checklist, accept the fact that this common condition now describes you. The sooner you admit this, the quicker you will begin the process of recovery.

Second, try to determine what is causing your depression. At times this will be easy, but often we cannot identify any cause. Sometimes we need a friend or counselor who can help us to spot losses, rejection, helplessness, hurt, anger, sin, guilt, low self-esteem, or other influences that may be triggering despair. Don't forget the possibility of physical causes. If depression persists, a good physical examination from a competent physician would be important.

Third, ponder what you can do about the causes of depression. If you have lost a loved one, are there ways in which you can "go on"? When there is guilt, why not confess to God and to others? If you feel helpless, are there some things that *can* be done to change a situation? And what about your perspective? Might there be value in "counting your blessings" and trying to see things positively? Philippians 4:8 can become your theme: Whatever is true, honorable, right, pure, lovely, of good repute, excellent, or worthy of praise, "let your mind dwell on these things."

Fourth, acknowledge your feelings and try to think realistically. There are few things more frustrating than to hear someone (including a writer, friend, or preacher) tell us to snap out of our depression. That cannot be done, and frustration is the inevitable result of trying. It is more realistic to admit your feelings, share them with a friend or counselor, ponder their source, and consider how your thinking or actions can be changed in ways that might alter the feelings.

All this is difficult to do alone, but with God we are never by ourselves. Prayer and confession to God, therefore, becomes a fifth way of handling the depression. Recognize that you might not feel like praying or reading the Bible, but in time these spiritual activities can reap great benefits in overcoming depression.

Sixth, consider contacting an understanding friend or counselor. Other human beings can give us support, encouragement, challenge, understanding, and a clearer perspective on our depression. Psalm 55:22 instructs us to "cast your burden on the Lord, and He will sustain you." Undoubtedly He sustains through the Holy Spirit (who is described in the New Testament as our helper and comforter), but might He also meet our needs through the counseling ministry of others?

Seventh, do not reject the value of antidepressant medication, given under the guidance of a physician. Under proper care there is little risk of addiction to these drugs, and often they can help us face our difficulties more realistically and effectively.

Finally, don't expect quick cures. Depression often takes a long time to conquer, and it is easy to get impatient or to conclude that you'll never get better. For most people, handling depression is draining and time-consuming, but the result can be great personal growth and increased maturity.

Like winters in the north, depression sometimes seems to drag on forever without much apparent change. But in time, with divine help, human guidance, and your persistent determination, the frozen darkness of despair can give way to the warm brightness of a meaningful, hopeful future. The psalmists who cried to God "out of the depths" and waited for the Lord to act were soon expressing hope and praise (Psalm 69, 130). "Weeping may last for the night," state the Scriptures, but "joy comes in the morning" (Psalm 30:5). This is good to remember—especially in the winter of depression.

5

HOW TO HANDLE
impatience

Perhaps nothing separates the generations like our tastes in music. I try to appreciate the musical preferences of my teenage daughters (and some of those rock and country songs really *are* enjoyable). But to my middle-aged ear, much contemporary music sounds noisy, dissonant, repetitious, and filled with lyrics that are fixated on immorality and sadness. For some reason it also is supposed to be loud—very loud!

Why, I wonder, do they no longer write ballads like we had back in the good old days of the forties and fifties? Why do my kids howl in laughter when I give renditions of "Jeepers Creepers," "Three Little Fishes Swimming in the Brook", "Swinging on a Star," and other classics? Some of those old songs even had thought-provoking messages!

For example you may remember:

Patience and fortitude,
Patience and fortitude,
Patience and fortitude,
And things will be all right.

Even if we remembered the tune, most of us wouldn't sing that song today. The message seems so outdated, perhaps even un-American. In our modern Western world hardly anybody believes that patience is desirable. We are much more impressed with speed and efficiency. If there is anything we don't value, it surely is patience and fortitude.

Sometimes, however, we are forced to wait, and for many of us this is almost intolerable. Few things annoy us like traffic tie-ups, bureaucratic red tape, and the nonarrival of some important letter. Everybody knows that in traffic jams or at airline ticket counters the line you're not in is the line that moves fastest. This causes some people to spend half their lives darting back and forth from one line to another, and I cannot deny that I sometimes do this myself.

Recently in our local supermarket I watched a man who clearly was in a hurry. He had only a few items in his hand, but his whole manner radiated impatience. Shifting his weight from foot to foot, casting sharp glances at the other check-out lines, shaking his head, mumbling in frustration, biting his lip, looking disgusted and annoyed, this shopper was a living example of the dictionary definition of impatience: "uneasy, intolerant, and unwilling to be kept waiting." We had completed our shopping at the same time, but he was still waiting impatiently in the "fast service" line as I paid the bill and pushed our cart full of groceries out to the parking lot.

I have since thought about that man. Why was he so impatient? Was there a good reason for him to be in such a hurry? Did his impatience spill over into his manner of driving when he finally left the store with his purchases?

Psychology books, at least the ones in my library, almost never mention impatience, even though this is one of the biggest struggles that we modern people face, surrounded as we are by the hustle and bustle of contemporary living. In contrast, the ancient biblical writers mentioned impatience frequently. Often they instructed us to wait, and they have given many exhortations to be patient.

But how do we do this? How do we handle our tendencies to be impatient? How do we stay relaxed and unruffled when we're in a hurry? Part of the answer comes from looking at the reasons why so many of us get impatient in the first place.

First, *we are taught to be impatient.* Parents and teachers constantly encourage young people to "hurry up" or "quit dawdling." There may be some good reasons for this prodding; every parent knows that children aren't innately inclined to hurry. Eventually, however, most of our offspring learn to be like us, intolerant of delays and frustrated when forced to wait.

Have you ever traveled in countries where people are less concerned about time? A couple of years ago I visited South America and soon learned that in that great continent almost nothing starts at the stated hour. One night I was scheduled to speak at a meeting beginning at 7 P.M. My host picked me up at 6:45, but instead of rushing to the meeting site, we went out to eat. An hour or so later we reached the auditorium, which was still half empty because most people had not yet arrived.

How different this is from our culture! I don't like to arrive even two minutes late for a class, and can be mildly annoyed if a concert or church service doesn't start exactly on time. Mine is the thinking of a North American who has learned to be time-conscious—and impatient.

Once we learn, *we encourage one another to be impatient.* We admire punctuality, value good organization and time management, condemn ourselves when we procrastinate or are late, and sometimes complain about wasting too much time. We expect "on the spot, up to date" reports from the news media, and we want the pollsters and computers to give us election results even before people vote. College students sometimes try to hurry through school, and are praised when they rise rapidly in the professional or business world following graduation.

Even the church gets involved. We admire rapid church growth, we like to hear of numerous conversions overseas, and we get impatient when our spiritual growth is slow.

Have you ever heard the following little phrase?

Only one life, 'twill soon be past.
Only what's done for Christ will last.

This couplet can urge us to evaluate life's goals and priorities, but it also encourages us to hurry. Life will soon be over! There may be no tomorrow! We must be diligent and even impatient in serving the Lord!

This brings us to a third source of impatience. At least to some extent I suspect that *we have a natural bent toward impatience*. I can't prove this, and I don't know of any research reports to back up this conclusion. Isn't it interesting, however, that the Bible urges us to be patient, to "show forbearance," to be stedfast, to endure, wait, and persevere? Surely we have all these admonitions because of our fallen nature which creates a natural tendency to do the opposite—to be impatient and sometimes impulsive because we can't wait.

One of the greatest saints in all the Bible was Abraham. Even today he is admired by Jews, Christians, Muslims, and many who aren't especially inclined to be religious.

Abraham was rich, successful in his business, and deeply religious. He believed that God would be true to his promise of giving Abraham and Sarah a son, but the couple got impatient. When Abraham was eighty-six and Sarah was in her midseventies—well beyond menopause—they decided to take matters into their own hands. At his wife's urging, Abraham impregnated Sarah's Egyptian maid who subsequently bore a male child.

At first this seemed like a good plan, an effective way to hurry God along and get things done. But the blessed event was followed by marital friction, tension in the home, and conflict between the young mother and the aging Sarah. The end result of Abraham's impatience was stress, immorality, immaturity, and intolerance.

God helped the family straighten things out, and He forgave Abraham for his impatience. Then do you remember what happened?

Nothing!

For fourteen years Abraham and Sarah waited, still without children. They might have been in a hurry, but God was not. He showed the patience that Abraham lacked.

Phillips Brooks was a great New England preacher noted

for his poise and quiet manner. One day, however, a friend saw him impatiently pacing the floor like a caged lion.

"What's the trouble, Mr. Brooks?" the friend asked.

"The trouble," replied the preacher, "is that I'm in a hurry, but God isn't!"

Abraham and Sarah must have felt this way at times, and so have most of us. But just as we learn to be impatient, so we can learn patience.

We learn patience first by changing our attitudes and the ways in which we look at life. How many times have you been caught in traffic and become aware that your stomach has tightened up, your muscles are tense, and your attitude is one of irritability and frustration? When some impatient motorist drives in a cloud of dust along the shoulder of the road, we respond with both anger and secret admiration. If he tries to get back into the lane later, how easy it is to look straight ahead and gleefully refuse to give him a space—all because we are annoyed by the delay and his brashness.

In such situations we create a lot of our own tensions by our attitudes. What is to be gained by getting angry or noncooperative? What can be accomplished by worrying? Isn't it better to look at the delay more realistically: "I'm caught in traffic. There's nothing I can do about it, so I might as well relax."

Talking to ourselves like this can have a great calming effect, especially if we do it so often that it becomes a way of life. Criticizing others and complaining about circumstances accomplishes nothing except to get us stirred up with anger and bogged down with bitterness.

The story is told of one recent U.S. president who liked to call the vice-president to come immediately, but when the vice-president hurriedly arrived at the Oval Office, he was kept waiting. Instead of getting mad (some have wondered if that's what the president wanted), the vice-president always brought something useful to do while he waited.

You might try this next time you are kept waiting for an appointment. Try to maintain a gracious attitude and think of useful things to do. Try praying, thinking through plans for the future, or reading (which, of course, isn't recommended in traffic). This can keep you from getting angry and more impatient.

To change our thinking like this isn't easy, especially when we've spent a lifetime learning to be impatient. Most of us discover, therefore, that *we really only learn patience by seeking and expecting divine help.*

The apostle James describes the farmer who plants seed and then must wait until the crop grows and matures. In the same way, we are exhorted to be patient (James 5:7–8).

This message is repeated throughout the New Testament. The "worthy life" is characterized by patience and a lack of complaints or griping. When persecution and great turmoil enter our lives, we are forced to be patient, but this brings growth and greater joy (James 1:2–4; Eph. 4:1–2; Col. 1:10–12).

According to the Bible, Christians are expected to be patient, but this comes not by human willpower. We develop patience as God's Holy Spirit works in our lives to bring peace and to make us more Christlike (Col. 3:12–15; Eph. 6:22).

We can ask God to bring the patience that He desires, and we can expect that He will answer. Remember, however, that this prayer may not be answered quickly. Sometimes He gives us patience by making us wait.

Abraham learned this, but I still wonder about that man in the supermarket. Will he go through life perpetually uptight and impatient?

Most people are familiar with the famous prayer of Reinhold Niebuhr:

God grant me serenity
To accept the things I cannot change,
Courage to change the things I can
And wisdom to know the difference.

Maybe something like that was in the mind of the person who wrote the old song about patience and fortitude. The words didn't carry much of a biblical message, but there was wisdom in the lyrics nevertheless. Life *is* a lot smoother when we learn to relax, with God's help, and to wait patient-ly.

6

HOW TO HANDLE
family tensions

At some time, I suspect, every psychologist comes up with one or two laws of human behavior. After a year of deliberation, I have decided that my first law will be as follows:

> "When a kid has a paper route, the parents also have a paper route."

Clearly this isn't as earth-shattering as Ohm's law or the Peter Principle, but for me it is more meaningful than the first law of thermodynamics or the laws of gravity (which sometimes cause newspapers to fall, not where I aim them, but in the mud and among thorny bushes).

About a year ago my youngest daughter decided to deliver the weekly Lake Zurich *Lakes Countryside,* and I started thinking about my law. After observing her sister's first paycheck or two, our other daughter applied for a paper route as well, and now every Thursday, rain or shine (it usually rains), the papers get folded and delivered, always with some parental help since the routes are several miles from home or school and too far away to be reached by bicycle. Whenever someone gets sick we all pitch in to get the papers out, and when the weather is especially bad we drive the car around the route.

In one sense, these paper routes have become an opportunity for family togetherness—something like attending church, wandering around shopping centers, or going to the emergency room for X-rays when somebody falls off a skateboard. Judging from the current flood of articles, seminars, and books on the family, however, such togetherness is becoming more and more rare. Some have argued that the family is changing radically, and according to a recent Census Bureau report only 13 percent of all family units now consist of the traditional working father and homemaker mother living together with their children. The prevalence of childless marriages, single-parent families, communes, families where both parents work, and a variety of other living arrangements all demonstrate that family living is in flux.

Much of this change in the family has taken place within the last half-century. As a nation we have become much more mobile, and since people move more frequently; much traditional family closeness and solidarity have been abandoned. Television and other media influences have exploded into our lives and living rooms, teaching values and attitudes that can undermine family togetherness and encourage declining morals and marital infidelity. The divorce rate has been soaring, along with child abuse, mate beating, and even the physical mistreatment of older parents by their adult children. All this reflects the conflict and violence that seem to have taken over in many homes. While most of us get tired of hearing that the family is in trouble, we know that to ignore such evidence is to hide from cancerous influences which can subtly undermine even the best Christian homes.

What can we do to handle family tensions and build stronger homes? Some suggestions might be helpful.

Make the family a priority. Several years ago I was invited to speak at the annual family conference of a large California church. The meetings began on Mother's Day and my first talk was about family togetherness. As I stood in front of that huge congregation, however, I was struck with the fact that in order to give a speech on building families, I had left my own wife and children in another part of the country to celebrate Mother's Day alone.

How easy it is to let our marriages and families slip into a place of secondary importance! Busy with building our careers, molding a ministry, making money, or even working in the church and community, we ignore family members or subtly push them aside. We may have every intention of taking care of family needs later, but often they get left forever because we find it more challenging, important, or fun to be involved in other things.

As far as I can tell, God called me to be a writer, teacher, and psychologist. But he also called me to be a husband, father, and son. To build my career or satisfy my social needs while overlooking my family is both disobedient and sinful. Periodically we each need to ponder God's will for our families and seek his guidance as we strive to put our family responsibilities in a place of prime importance. When we do this, the family can become an exciting part of our lives, rather than a collection of demanding relatives who pull us away from more pleasant activities.

Work to build a balanced life. I once was asked to write an article on "How to live a balanced life." Writing the article was a challenge; putting my conclusions into practice has been even harder.

Most of us have a number of pressures, demands, and responsibilities that cry out for our time and energy. After we go to work, attend church, and try to do routine duties at home, we find that little time is left for rest, relaxation, Christian service, or quality time with the family. This surely was a problem Jesus understood.

In the midst of His earthly ministry the Lord was very busy. The first chapter of Mark describes a day in which He taught, worshipped, healed, and made important decisions. Then in the evening when He might have wanted to rest, "the whole city" gathered at His door, bringing people who were sick and in need of help. Undoubtedly Jesus worked until late at night, but the next day "in the early morning, while it was still dark, He arose and went out and departed to a lonely place," where He could pray, communicate with His

Father, and perhaps prepare for the day ahead. When the disciples found Him, Jesus gently refused to be swayed by the demands of the crowds. He had pulled away, thought through his priorities, made plans, and now was ready to move to the next task.

It takes time for such planning, discipline for such living, and a flexibility that enables us to "hang loose" when we are faced with the unexpected. Most of us know the importance of getting sufficient rest, eating a balanced diet, finding time for exercise, and pulling away for periods of meditation. But these things get pushed aside when we are faced with the pressures of everyday living. It may be that you have discovered, as I have, that unless we schedule time for Bible reading it rarely gets done. Unless we deliberately take time for family members, their needs get overlooked as we are involved in more pressing issues. Once again we are faced with the issue of priorities. What we really think is important gets done. Who we think is important gets our attention.

On occasion I have met pastors whose families resent both the church and the ministry because these seem to have stolen away the head of the home. I do not want my wife and children to resent my work, so I try to let them know what I do, involve them whenever possible in my activities, find time to be with them without hurrying, and give them the freedom and encouragement to do what interests them. By sharing a sincere interest in each other's activities, we are learning to understand one another better, to live lives that are more balanced and less me-centered, and to be less dominated by the workaholic mentality.

Work on communication. Every counselor knows that communication is at the core of good marriage and family relationships. Husbands, wives, and children must listen carefully to each other, express their thoughts and feelings clearly, and work at mutual understanding. We must recognize that family members sometimes communicate in nonverbal ways—by tears, outbursts of anger, withdrawal, and other subtle messages. We must realize that family communication involves time, commitment, and a willingness to be confronted and to confront in a spirit of love and mutual respect. Poor communication and family tensions often go together.

Recognize the value of family clusters. There was a time in our history when people rarely moved and individuals grew up surrounded by parents, grandparents, cousins, aunts, uncles, and a host of other relatives. But for many of us things have changed. In our mobile society, families have become scattered, and it is common to find people who live hundreds of miles from the nearest relative. When crises arise there are no family members to give encouragement and guidance, or provide babysitting. Family holidays like Thanksgiving and Christmas are spent alone, far away from traditional celebrations. Children grow up apart from grandparents and away from cousins, aunts, or uncles.

Just as individuals need other individuals, however, so do families need other families. To meet this need, many families have formed clusters—the informal joining of families with other families for mutual support, encouragement, learning, help, and times of fun. These clusters may consist of people from within a neighborhood, or groups from one's church. Sometimes members of Bible study groups get together with their entire families for picnics, potlucks, and other social gatherings. Such gatherings let families observe other families, and the benefits can be even greater when the cluster includes older couples, singles, and students away from home, as well as the more traditional mother-father-children combination.

The family should be a place where we can relax, discover how to get along with each other, learn to care, and find a haven from the pressures of life. Within the family, people of all ages should learn about God, about right or wrong, and about the importance of honesty, self-respect, hard work, and other traditional values. The family should provide support in times of crisis and rejoicing when things are going well.

We're learning these things in our family—even though we have a long way to go. When I as a husband and father started taking more time with my family members, everybody relaxed and we began to really enjoy each other. Deep within me I harbor the hope that someday we'll even think it's fun to deliver our papers together.

7

HOW TO HANDLE
communication
breakdowns

The first new car I ever owned was a Volkswagen. It was light green with beige upholstery and, in those bachelor days, I cared for it like a baby.

One day, at a busy intersection, my little "bug" and I had a run-in with a big Lincoln Continental. I'm not sure what caused the accident, but some things do remain clearly in my memory: the demolished front of my car, the contrasting scratch on the Lincoln, and the hostility of the other driver. He pulsated with anger, shook his fist, hollered, and called me names. My stunned response was to suggest quietly that we call the police and file our accident report so the man could be on his way as soon as possible.

Perhaps my reaction came as a surprise because my new-found acquaintance quickly calmed down. Before long he was even picking up some of the debris, and he offered to give me a ride (since it was obvious that I no longer had any means of transportation). After watching all this from the gathering crowd of onlookers, a friend later reminded me of Proverbs 15:1: "A gentle answer turns away wrath." But gentle answers are not always apparent when people try to communicate, especially if there is frustration or major differences of opinion. More often there is misunderstanding, hurt feelings, confusion, and sometimes even sarcasm and name calling.

Good communication takes time and effort. It also takes

skill, and most often it comes when we remember some basic guidelines for getting along with others. Periodically it can be helpful to check on our communication. Ask yourself the following questions, especially when there is conflict at work, in your home, in your neighborhood, or at church.

Do I really want to communicate? Have you ever listened to preschool children talking to one another? First one talks and then the other, but often they are not even discussing the same topic. There is little listening and even less real communication—unless, of course, they get into a fight.

We adults are sometimes like preschoolers. We fail to realize that communication involves a sincere desire to understand and to be understood. We are more interested in pushing our opinions on to someone else than we are in really sharing. When there are communication breakdowns and impasses, perhaps we should begin by asking, "Do I really want to communicate, or am I more concerned with forcing my viewpoint on to someone else?"

Do I listen carefully? This is the first lesson that counselors learn, and it is a valuable principle of communication for all of us: Learn to listen carefully, don't interrupt, and try to understand what the other person is saying. This isn't easy, especially in the heat of an argument when we feel attacked and when we want to defend ourselves.

Sometimes tempers calm down considerably when we stop and calmly say something like the following: "Let me make sure I understand. Are you saying. . .?" Then try to summarize the other person's position. To do this, you have to start listening carefully.

Do I concentrate on getting and stating facts? Sometimes we make statements that are more an indication of our feelings than a reflection of facts. Have you ever had the experience of exploding in anger at one of your children, only to discover later that you blamed the wrong person? Besides making one feel sheepish, the experience provides a time for saying,

"I'm sorry." It also is a reminder that we should look for facts before we leap toward another with accusations and criticisms.

Do I use emotionally explosive words? Some words are like triggers on guns. When you use them, an explosion almost always follows. Consider, for example, what happens when you use words like "you never . . ." or "you always. . . ." In all likelihood the sentence that follows will only be partially true, but it can trigger anger and a defensive reaction.

Communication problems rarely are solved when we use ridicule, name calling, interrupting, sarcasm, criticism, or words that tend to "put down" the other person so that he or she is made to feel guilty, manipulated, or inferior. Do you remember the man whose Lincoln collided with my Volkswagen? He demonstrated that a gentle answer—spoken in a gentle way and with gentle words—can do much to tone down wrath and build smoother communication. It has been suggested that "never raise your voice" can be a good guideline for calming interpersonal tension.

Do I state my position clearly? At times we don't communicate because we don't say what we really think or mean. In popular terms this is called "beating around the bush." It is a practice which rarely builds good communication.

There is, of course, a place for tact and the use of carefully chosen words by which we can speak the truth, as we see it, *in love.* In doing this, try to bring up the problems that bother you even if these might create tension temporarily.

Do I send double messages? We have all heard that actions speak louder than words, but what happens if the words and actions send different messages? I can tell my children, "I love you. You are very important to me," but these words are pretty empty if my actions say, "Don't bother me—I'm too busy!"

Early in my teaching career, a student came to talk about

her beliefs. "I'm sick of Christianity," she proclaimed. "My father is a pious pillar in the church who is respected by the pastor and known to be a denominational leader. But at home he has no time for the kids, mistreats my mother, and apart from 'family devotions' shows none of the religious front that he puts on in church."

This father was giving a double message. His words were honoring Christ, but his actions were not. And the daughter was more impressed with his actions.

Until and unless someone points this out, we may not even realize that we are saying one thing and giving another message by our actions. Recognize that family members and friends may be experts on our behavior. They see us every day, and we must resist the tendency to dismiss their observations quickly—especially when there is a possibility that they might be right! If they think we are giving double messages, they probably are right.

Do I realize that there may be honest differences in opinion and experience? Every issue can be seen from different points of view. My children, for example, have views about rock music that differ from the perspective of their more sedate parents. To build good communication, it is important that we recognize these differences and try to understand each other's viewpoint. Such an attitude can facilitate communication and avoid unnecessary confrontation.

Do I show an uncooperative, combative attitude? Repeatedly the Bible talks about love. It is the most prominent mark of a Christian, and it should characterize our attitudes and contacts with others. When we are determined to fight and argue, however, miscommunication is inevitable. When we honestly try to be loving, we get along better.

And what does it mean to be loving? I Corinthians 13 talks about this. Love, or love communication, is patient, kind, nonboastful, not rude or self-seeking, not easily angered; it is the kind of communication that is trusting and persevering.

Do I accept personality differences in others? Recently I had problems with a tape recorder, so I took it to the repair shop. The man across the counter was pleasant but gruff. "What kind of tapes do you use in this thing?" he growled. "They must be made of sandpaper considering the condition of this machine! And I suppose you never clean the heads? Most people don't."

My first impulse was to take the machine, run to my car, and cower in guilt because of my tape recorder abusing. I had to recognize, however, that this was the repairman's way of relating. It wasn't pleasant, but it wasn't worth getting upset about. I joked with him briefly and then left.

Sometimes we encounter people whose personalities are abrasive and seemingly unchangeable. What we cannot change gently, we can learn to accept. Communication requires flexibility and willingness to overlook personality quirks. That takes determination and maturity, but then so does good communication.

When we aren't communicating, it isn't always easy to remember principles such as those that we have outlined. At times we all fail, but when this happens we can determine to do better next time. It may help to remember that communication breakdowns are not something new. The Bible is filled with examples of people who couldn't get along with each other. But this is one of the reasons why Jesus came to this earth: to break down the partitions that divide us and to make us all one in Christ Jesus. That is a reachable goal. It starts with Him, working in us, to build better communication with each other.

8

HOW TO HANDLE
weariness

When I was a boy, autumn was my favorite season. I liked the changing leaves, the crisp mornings, Halloween, my annual birthday party, and even (for a week or two) the return to school.

Now that I am older, I still like the fall, but these last months of the year arouse different thoughts. I try to ignore my birthday, and Halloween has ceased to be a big issue since the time, two years ago, when my wife and I stayed up half the night making a costume for our daughter who wanted to dress up like a bottle of Dr. Pepper. (She wore the costume only briefly and took it off because it was too confining.)

As autumn fades and winter approaches, I now tend to think about football and Christmas—both of which make me tired. As I watch the NFL, it can be tiring just seeing those padded combatants plow into each other in battle over the possession of a piece of pigskin.

Like football, Christmas begins in August, at least in the stores near our house. Unlike football, however, Christmas is not a spectator sport. By mid-December almost everyone is caught up in such frenzy that we forget the real meaning of the celebration and sometimes start the new year too tired to pack away the decorations.

With all these activities, late fall seems to be a time of special weariness, in spite of the fun. Perhaps there are people—like politicians, workaholics, or even a few football players—who have endless vitality, boundless energy, and the ability to get along with only snatches of sleep. But most of us aren't like that. Even when we seem to be getting enough rest, we experience periods of fatigue, a condition Dr. Dwight Carlson defines as a "lack of energy, weariness, tiredness . . . no ambition, no interest, lack of pep," and a feeling of being "all in."

How do we handle such weariness? Let's begin with the most obvious solution.

Get some rest. The traditional eight hours of sleep is not necessary for everyone, but we all need at least some uninterrupted periods of rest and rejuvenation. "It is vain for you to rise up early, to retire late," the psalmist wrote (Psalm 127:2).

To be effective, not all our sleep must be taken at night, stretched out on a comfortable bed. Winston Churchill was known as a "dedicated catnapper" whose brief daytime naps renewed his mind and body for the evening's work. At least three recent presidents—Truman, Kennedy, and Johnson—took midday naps, and so, I have noticed, do some of my students when we gather for classes after lunch.

Some people sleep too much, at times because of laziness or boredom, but often because sleep is a way of avoiding stress, depression, or other pressures of life. Oversleepers often feel sluggish for the entire day. They are too tired to be alert; they are weary because of oversleep.

Then there are people who have the opposite problem, insomnia. It's helpful to get up at a regular time in the morning, to avoid stimulating discussions or reading before turning out the light at night, and to resist the temptation to eat heavily late in the evening. Learning to deal with our worries during the day, and even drinking a glass of warm milk can help us settle down and drift into sleep. Sleeping pills can help as well, but these are best taken only under the guidance of a physician.

Get some exercise. About two years ago I went to my doctor with complaints of being tired all the time. "Probably there's something wrong with my blood," I thought while sitting in the waiting room. "Maybe I've got mononucleosis or perhaps I've been working too hard."

The physical examination revealed, however, that I was a healthy specimen who spent too much time sitting behind a desk.

"Get some exercise," my doctor recommended. "If you don't want to jog, buy an exerciser bicycle and ride it regularly."

Such advice is supported by a host of physical fitness experts whose research has demonstrated the need for regular muscular activity. This keeps the body in shape, prevents the muscles from getting flabby or sluggish, helps us release pent-up anxieties or frustrations, and as a result, enables us to win over weariness.

Watch your diet. The radio advertisement for blue jeans for men says, "Let's face it, as you get older your body shape changes. Flat stomachs and slim hips are for teenagers, but men over thirty have a different build."

That's an understatement. A government report recently concluded that at least one American adult in four is more than twenty percent overweight. Some of these people snack too much, or fill up on hamburgers, french fries, and other high-carbohydrate foods which are washed down with chocolate milkshakes or sugary soft drinks, and topped off with a chocolate bar. When the pounds increase, we jump into a variety of fad diets, many of which can leave us physically run down. A balanced diet can do wonders to help banish fatigue.

Check your health. About 10 percent of the time, according to one estimate, fatigue means there is a more serious problem. Infections, endocrine disorders, anemia, and a variety of other disorders can drain us physically and signal that something is wrong with the body. At such times a doctor's examination is needed, but prepare yourself for a nonmedical diagnosis. The physician may suggest that your weariness comes primarily from stress.

Reduce your stresses. People who write about fatigue sometimes describe what has come to be known as the "tired housewife syndrome," a condition seen in homemakers who are overworked, depressed, erratic in their eating habits, lacking in exercise, bored, sometimes disorganized, and perpetually fatigued. Many of these women are genuinely worn out, but according to one physician they also are *4-F females*: furious, frantic, futile, and frustrated. Like their stress-driven husbands and anxious children, these women are tired because of the awesome power of daily stress.

Sometimes stress is best managed through the help of a competent counselor. Often, however, we can reduce our own stresses by: trying to uncover, eliminate, or reduce the causes of stress; finding a time and place to retreat, meditate and relax; pausing to get a more realistic perspective on life; and seeking God's guidance as we attempt to cope more effectively.

We must be alert to the tension produced by noise. An evening in a crowded restaurant with a loud singer and back-up band in the nearby lounge is no way to relax. Nor is Christmas shopping in a bustling mall, decorated with flashing lights and enlivened by catchy seasonal music. We live in a stimulus-saturated society which constantly increases our stress levels and makes coping more difficult. Sometimes we need peace and quiet more than anything else, even if this means retreating to a nearby library or into the bathtub.

Ponder your emotions. Anxiety can wear us out. Feelings of boredom, discouragement, failure, inadequacy, and uselessness are all draining, and so is the pain of loneliness. So often do these emotions accompany weariness that it can be difficult to know which comes first—our frustrated feelings or our fatigue.

Feelings are God-created and a part of being human, and

useful for releasing tension, giving excitement to life, and warning of problems. Even happiness and enthusiasm can be wearing (as some people discover each Christmas), and so, of course, can sadness or disappointment. There is value in asking, "What emotions am I feeling?" "Why do I feel as I do?" "How can I change my behavior and thinking so that I feel differently?" A friend can help as you ponder these questions and try to make changes in your life.

Recognize your attitudes. Have you known people whose lives are characterized by bitterness and anger? Such people are to be pitied. They often are rejected (nobody likes to be around sour people), unhappy, and tired because so much energy is consumed on their negative get-even mentality.

Bitterness is not the only fatigue-producing attitude. Sometimes weariness comes to people who:

• are rigid, compulsive, and so intent on pleasing others that they can't relax;

• are workaholics, some of whom are dedicated Christians, pushing themselves without relief but wondering why their bodies slow down and their efficiency wanes;

• are plagued by so much guilt and feelings of inadequacy that they always feel driven to make up for their assumed failures;

• are so intent on playing a role that they can't let down their masks and permit others to see them as they really are; or

• are so intent on acquiring success, wealth, or possessions that there is time for nothing else.

At times perhaps many of us are tempted to each of these attitudes. Whenever they appear they must be faced honestly, committed to God, and actively resisted (with a counselor's help when necessary).

Consider, for example, those who weary themselves in the pursuit of money. They need to change their attitudes, pondering the biblical writer's comments:

"Do not weary yourself to gain wealth, Cease from your

consideration of it. When you set your eyes on it, it is gone. For wealth certainly makes itself wings" (Prov. 23:4,5).

Evaluate your spirituality. The Scriptures confirm that weariness comes from a variety of causes including anger (Jer. 6:11), fear (Psalm 69:1–3), the striving for wealth (Prov. 23:4), travel (John 4:6), and even because of an excessive devotion to books (Eccl. 12:12). It also is possible to grow weary through doing good and getting involved in acts of compassion (Gal. 6:9).

When such weariness arises, we can help one another with good deeds (Gal. 6:9) and words of encouragement (Is. 50:4). Both the giving and the accepting of help can be beneficial when we are tired.

Ultimately, however, we must bring our weariness to the Lord in prayer. In deeply reassuring terms, Jesus arged His weary followers to come to Him, to learn from Him, and to experience the rest which He alone can give (Matt. 11:28–30). Such a promise echos one of the best-known quotations in the Old Testament. God is never tired, we read in the book of Isaiah. He gives strength and power to the weary, and promises that those who "wait for the Lord will gain new strength; they will mount up with wings like eagles, they will run and not get tired, they will walk and not become weary."

When my wife and I got married, some friends gave us a wall plaque with these famous words from Isaiah 40:28–31. The plaque hangs in our kitchen. Its ancient biblical prophecy applies even now.

9

HOW TO HANDLE
spiritual dryness

On a trip to a tropical island, Britain's Prince Charles was once offered a sample of the local thirst quencher. After swallowing a mouthful, the prince reportedly gulped, smiled weakly, and exclaimed, "It's amazing the things I do for the sake of England!"

For some reason I thought about the prince's remark during a visit last summer to Six Flags, an amusement park with acres of rides, shows, and souvenir stands. We were on a family vacation and discovered that all attractions at the park were free, after paying about ten dollars each to get in. When we went through the gate I announced that I would not be going on any of the rides. That was a vain hope. By four o'clock, in response to youthful urgings, I had been tilted, flipped, and juggled innumerable times, all for the cause of family togetherness. As I dangled in the air, floating down to earth from the Parachute Drop, I thought, "It's amazing the things I do for the sake of fatherhood!"

Perhaps most people who visit amusement parks go looking for fun. In watching the crowds at Six Flags, however, I wondered why so many of the people looked sad, in spite of all the entertainment opportunities and thrill-producing rides. For many, I suspect, life is like riding the Screaming Eagle roller coaster. There is anticipation, fear, a few jolts, some high points, brief excitement, and a quick return to the normal routines of life.

This is true even for Christians. We like to think that our lives are different (and often they are), but for most of us there are days or even months when we trudge through discouragement, unhappiness, listlessness, and feelings of inefficiency.

These feelings can indicate a state that Walter Trobisch has called "spiritual dryness." It is a time in life when the living God seems dead. We read the Bible, but it doesn't say much. We may go to church, but the services seem routine and meaningless. Our devotional life becomes an empty habit. Our consciences become dull and insensitive. Instead of joy we have discouragement and apathy. In place of an interest in spiritual things we feel indifference and boredom. Rather than enthusiasm we experience fatigue. There is little desire to "serve the Lord with gladness."

Before long, we begin asking troublesome questions. Why don't I sense any joy? Have I lost my love for the Lord? Has God forsaken me? Why is my spiritual life so dead, my prayers so empty, and my attitude to Christian things so indifferent?

While spiritual dryness is common, it is not the normal state for a Christian. We should seek to overcome such barren times, and we can do so by pondering the following ten questions:

Am I a believer? A lot of people attend church and do good deeds, but they are nonbelievers. They have never acknowledged that Christ is Lord or asked Him to forgive their sins. Such people, according to the Bible, are spiritually dead. Since they are lifeless, it is impossible for them to escape spiritual dryness until they experience the new life that comes from Christ. Like the father described in the Scripture, our first step to spiritual rejuvenation is to begin with a simple prayer: "Jesus, I do believe; help my unbelief."

Am I sinning? In recent years even psychologists have begun to talk about the reality of sin. This involves specific acts such as lying, stealing, or committing adultery, but ac-

cording to the Bible, sin involves much more. It is any attitude or action that goes against God's will. When we sin
consciously, fail to repent, and refuse to confess our faults to
God and to others, then spiritual dryness is certain to result.
"When I kept silent about my sin," King David wrote in
Psalm 32:3,4 "my body wasted away ... my vitality was
drained away as with the fever heat of summer."

Everybody sins, but some people fail to realize that
unconfessed sin is destructive and enslaving. Many do not
know or remember that if we confess our sins, Christ will
forgive and clean away all unrighteousness (I John 1:9). The
writer of Pslams discovered this. He confessed his sin, experienced God's forgiveness, and ended Psalm 32 with gladness,
rejoicing, and a shout of joy.

Am I out of shape physically? Many believers who seek to do
the will of God still experience spiritual dryness. Sometimes
the reason for this is physical. It is well known that we often
don't think clearly or act efficiently when we are tired, run-
down, overweight, not eating properly, or failing to get exercise. Simple as this may seem, it is possible that spiritual
dryness may in part result from a disregard of the body and
its physical needs.

Am I spiritually undernourished? About two years ago, I was
asked to write a book on counseling. The publisher gave me a
deadline, and I worked enthusiastically to finish the project
on time. For several months I worked twelve to fourteen
hours every day, stopping only for meals and a rest day each
Sunday.

Near the end of my work I sensed a lack of spiritual
vitality. I had become too busy to spend extended times in
prayer and Bible reading. In my writing, I was giving out
continuously, but I wasn't taking much in. It is not surprising
that spiritual dryness soon had me in its grasp.

Just as a baby never develops without nourishment, so
Christians cannot grow or experience vitality if they fail to
spend time in prayer, ignore the Bible, forsake worship ser-

vices, and spend so much time giving to others that they are never rejuvenated. Jesus recognized this clearly. Before and after periods of intensive work, He would withdraw for times of prayer and meditation before God. We must do the same if we are to avoid the dryness, spiritual indifference, and joyless routines which can affect even pastors and other religious leaders.

Am I spiritually overfed? At times we eat too much and then feel uncomfortable. It is difficult to eat with moderation at Thanksgiving or Christmas, and for some people, visits to amusement parks or fairs lead to the eating of junk food they could do without.

A similar condition can influence our spiritual lives. At times we fill our minds with junk ideas—thoughts, literature, or television and movie themes which are contrary to Christian teaching and thus disruptive spiritually. At other times, we fill our minds with good things, but because of our failure to share with others, we become spiritually bloated.

I see this often in my seminary students. They arrive on campus spiritually alert and ready to learn. Before long they are involved with a steady diet of Bible study, devotional reading, chapel services, and theological discussions. Like sponges, they soak up and retain everything, but eventually they become spiritually stuffed and lethargic.

The essence of Christianity is giving. While some Christians may be able to take in and retain unlimited quantities of spiritual food, most of us need to be sharing with others. Might it be that people who never give away money, time, energy, prayer support, and ideas are people who never grow spiritually?

Am I legalistic and hypercritical? Have you noticed how Jesus dealt with people? He always maintained His standards of right and wrong, but He showed compassionate understanding when people were uninformed, confused, repentant, and seeking to find answers to their questions. With the local religious leaders, however, Jesus was almost ruthless in His criticism. These leaders believed that spiritual dryness could be avoided by following rules or regulations, and Jesus clearly disagreed.

Obedience to rules can lead to pride and produce a "holier-than-thou" condemnation of others. The Christian does seek to live a life that is pleasing to God, but we must avoid three ways of thinking which can undermine us spiritually. First there is *legalism,* the making of rules which we expect ourselves and others to follow. Second is something called *gnosticism,* the belief that spirituality comes only to those with superior knowledge. Finally there is *asceticism,* the idea that spiritual dryness can only be avoided if we and others consciously deny pleasures and material things. These three ideas have little biblical support and often lead to frustration and self-centered attitudes of superiority.

Am I thinking clearly? Living in a non-Christian culture, it is difficult for us to avoid the nonbiblical attitudes of the people all around. Our society, for example, puts a high value on self-sufficiency, rugged individualism, and the acquisition of possessions and power. How easily we can become engulfed with such self-centered thinking as the struggle to get ahead, the drive to get more money, or the urge to get even and get noticed. When God is left out of our lives, these attitudes can become idols and ways of thinking that are inconsistent with biblical teaching. Without fail this leads to spiritual dryness.

Is my life unbalanced? A pastor once approached me at a conference to complain that his family life seemed to be falling apart. "I have always believed," he stated, "that if I take care of my ministry, God will take care of my family. But my family life is terrible, and this is influencing me spiritually."

Here was a dedicated believer who had become so engulfed in his work that life had become unbalanced. He had no time for his family. He rarely rested, avoided hobbies, ignored the need for vacations, and then wondered why he felt drained.

Spiritual dryness frequently comes when we get so involved with our work, sports, a hobby, church, our families, or some other aspect of life that other things are left out and life becomes unbalanced. For spiritual vitality and emotional health, we need a balance between work and rest, solitude and social involvement, individual and family activities, along with a willingness both to learn from others and to give creatively in return.

Am I spiritually powered? The Holy Spirit lives within believers and is available to teach, strengthen, and alert us to sin. But the Spirit can be ignored, quenched, or pushed aside. This leads inevitably to spiritual dryness, which is relieved as we repeatedly are filled with the Spirit (Eph.5:18). Such a filling comes whenever we examine ourselves, confess our sin, and ask the Holy Spirit to fill and control us. Surely this is a not a once-in-a-life-time event. It is something we do constantly. Emotional "highs" do not always follow, but in time we begin to see the slow development of love, peace, joy, patience, and the other spiritual characteristics which are the marks of a maturing believer.

Am I too independent? The Christian is part of a body or group of believers. We need each other and are responsible for mutual caring, helping, teaching, challenging, and support. When we ignore other believers, try to grow on our own, or get involved in climbing a status ladder, we are heading for spiritual dryness, because we have forsaken our brothers and sisters in violation of God's teaching.

In all this, we must remember that Christians are in a spiritual battle. The devil wants us to be confused, distressed, ineffective, and spiritually dry. His attacks, it seems, come regularly, but we are especially likely to fall when we are tired, not feeling well, emotionally drained, fresh from a spiritual mountain-top experience, or successful in some task.

The Christian, therefore, must be alert to spiritual dryness, but confident in God's power and in His desire to keep us moving spiritually.

Probably most people discover that their spiritual lives have both high and low points, but we need not soar and plummet like the riders on that amusement park roller coaster. Steady spiritual growth is more stable and less disruptive. It also is available for anyone who sincerely wants to avoid or overcome spiritual dryness.

10

HOW TO HANDLE
mental attitudes

How did I let myself get into this?

That question crossed my mind repeatedly as I watched the room fill with eager seminar participants, each clutching a notebook, a big manual, and a "free" ballpoint pen. There were almost two hundred of us taking our places around circular tables which had been set up in the ballroom of a large suburban hotel. In return for $100 each, we were about to experience two days of learning how to develop a positive mental attitude (something that everybody referred to as P.M.A.). As the seminar began, however, I realized that my mental attitude wasn't very positive. Seminars usually bore me, and I wasn't sure that I wanted to sit through several hours of enthusiastic rhetoric about how I should be a positive-possibility thinker.

In recent years a lot of emphasis has been placed on the value of positive thinking. Dr. Norman Vincent Peale, the famous New York pastor, has written widely and spoken all over the world about this. His book, *The Power of Positive Thinking*, has sold over two million copies and has been translated into more than thirty languages. More recently Dr. Robert Schuller has preached the possibility thinking message persuasively and graciously on a weekly, nationwide television program that originates from his large and growing church in California. Dozens of books have appeared on the subject of P.M.A., books written by both Christians and nonbelievers, and a host of seminars have been held similar to the one I attended.

It is true that negative thinking makes our lives miserable. People who constantly criticize and who always expect the worst rarely go through life with a happy disposition. It is easy for any of us to fall into the trap of bitterness, depair, fault-finding, or an attitude that assumes things will get worse. Sometimes our negative thinking even helps to bring about the things we dread. When we expect the worst, we do nothing to prevent our expectations from coming true.

Recently I was contemplating my role as the father of two young ladies who are entering the teenage years. At first I concluded: "These next few years are going to be very hard. I've never before had teenagers in my home. I know the problems that can arise. I'll never survive as a father."

But that was negative thinking of the worst kind, so I began to consider that while the teen years could be difficult, they also could be fun—for our whole family. Soon my attitude changed, the family relaxed, and we all agreed to experience the next decade as an adventure. My wife and I still are inexperienced in raising teenagers, but our attitude is positive, which is likely to help when we are called on to make difficult decisions as our girls move into adulthood.

But is P.M.A. the answer to negative thinking? Is a change in attitude the best way to deal with the stresses of life? Is positive thinking consistent with biblical teaching? I have pondered these and similar questions since taking the seminar and have reached several conclusions.

First, *P.M.A. can reduce pessimism and help us to cope with the pressures of life.* Do you remember the story of Pollyanna? In a book that first appeared in 1912, Eleanor Porter described the adventures of a little girl who saw the bright side of everything—even when she was mistreated by her stern aunt and struggling for her life following a serious auto accident. (The book grew out of a series of stories that originally appeared in Christian Herald.)

Today such thinking tends to be laughed at. We look with mild disdain on people who are "Pollyanna-ish" in their thinking. But perhaps Pollyanna had something that we modern adults lack. In some respects she was naive, but she had learned that a positive attitude brightens the one who possesses it, and makes things more pleasant for others as well. The apostle Paul said something similar when he wrote from the misery of a prison cell to the anxiety-plagued Philippians. He encouraged believers to "fix your thoughts on what is true and good and right. Think about things that are pure and lovely, and dwell on the fine, good things in others. Think about all you can praise God for and be glad about" (Phil. 4:8, LB).

Recently I read the story of a missionary who experienced a host of calamities within the period of a few weeks. Her mother and a close friend died on the same day, a family member was almost killed in a car accident, a son became seriously ill, and a flood ruined their home and most of their possessions—all while she and her family were living overseas, thousands of miles from relatives and friends who could give help and support. While she was struggling with discouragement and bitterness, the woman remembered that God wants us to give thanks in everything (I Thess. 5:18). She decided to look at her situation and find things for which she could still give thanks. This gave her a great lift—and started her on a practice of always looking for the good in the midst of the bad and thanking God. She also began to recognize that in God's overall plan for the world and for history, He will be victorious and will bring all things together for good. Looking at the world from this broader, divine perspective helped her to avoid pessimism and to effectively face the problems of life.

P.M.A. can also motivate us to action. Not long ago, somebody asked me why people are lazy. In attempting to find an answer I started looking into psychology books, but it soon became clear that most psychologists ignore laziness. (Perhaps this is a topic that mostly concerns parents and school teachers when they are trying to get kids moving.)

The lazy person doesn't want to make the effort needed to accomplish things in life. It seems easier and less risky to do as little as possible. When one is lazy, he or she may receive criticism from others, but this doesn't seem as bad as making the effort to do something that might bring failure or discomfort.

But isn't negative thinking the basis of laziness? "I'm no good," "I'll probably fail," "I can't do it" are pessimistic attitudes that keep us lazy, at least periodically. In contrast is the attitude expressed in the title of another book by Dr. Peale, *You Can If You Think You Can.* Motivated by this belief, thousands of people have overcome their lethargy, have refused to quit or to talk about defeat, and have gone on to accomplish great and significant things. History is filled with stories of people who persisted in spite of obstacles and temptations to quit. Such persistence is a distinguishing mark of successful people. Little wonder that *See You at the Top* is the title of one of the best-selling books on positive mental attitude.

This brings us to a third conclusion about positive thinking. In spite of its value, *P.M.A. can be harmful and can be applied toward anti-Christian purposes.*

Let's look first at its potential for harm. By looking at things optimistically, it is possible to overlook real danger and to miss seeing severe problems. In the Old Testament, a series of prophets announced God's judgment and called generations of rebellious people to repentance. But the prophets were often ignored or persecuted. Their hearers preferred to see things positively and to ignore the evidence that showed decline in society and sin in the people.

How many of us do this today? Positive about their work, many men fail to see that their marriages are falling apart—until it is too late. Thinking positively about our capabilities, many of us fail to acknowledge our sin and our need for a savior. Enthusiastic about our church programs, we do not see the spiritual and personal needs of hurting people in our midst. Often without our conscious awareness, positive thinking becomes a smoke screen which hides reality, enables us to deny our weaknesses, and provides an excuse for doing nothing about problems that may, in time, be destructive.

We must also face the fact that P.M.A. can be used in an unbiblical context. If our motives in possibility thinking are simply to propel ourselves to the top, then we have fallen victim to a humanistic way of life. If we fail to consider God's approval or help, then P.M.A. becomes evil.

Such thinking also ignores the issue of God's will for our lives. Jesus reminded His disciples that apart from Him they could do nothing (John 15:5). God does not want us to have a positive mental attitude that ignores Him and sends us off on our own self-centered schemes to get ahead. He wants obedience, a sensitivity to His leading, and a recognition of the sin and realities of life. He wants us to develop the attitude of a servant (Matt. 20:25–28), recognizing that this may not lead to a life of ease, acclaim, and positive thinking.

Where does this leave us? Suppose we agree that a positive mental attitude can reduce pessimism, help us deal with pressure, and motivate us away from laziness. Assume further that we agree that a positive mental attitude can be harmful, humanistic, and anti-Christian. How then do we think? How do we handle our mental attitudes?

Our mental attitude must be realistic, balanced, and biblically based. More than anyone else, the Christian has a reason for hope. We know that God loves us, values us, cares for us, and has prepared a place for us in His presence after this earthly life is over. The God who created the world and us still is in control, holding all things together by His power (Col. 1:17; Heb. 1:3). With this knowledge, Christians have every reason to shun pessimism and to think positively—about themselves, about the world in which we live, and about the future. This is P.M.A. based on the truths of divine revelation rather than on the "psyched-up" enthusiasm of self-development speakers.

The Bible is realistic. It warns of dangers, alerts us to the reality of sin, and teaches us about obedience. It calls us to repentance and commitment, shows that we are powerless apart from God, teaches the demands of discipleship, and realistically points out that the believer may be persecuted. It demonstrates that some of history's greatest saints—Jeremiah, John the Baptist, and Paul, for example—did not "make it to the top" even though they served God diligently and sought to act and think in accordance with His will.

Perhaps believers should not strive for a positive mental attitude. Instead we need what might be called C.M.A.—a Christian mental attitude. Such a perspective recognizes that God is sovereign, forgiving, compassionate, and concerned about individuals. *With Him,* all things are possible—even things that are impossible with humans (Matt. 19:26). The Christian's responsibility is to yield to God's control and direction, knowing that He will give us a realistic-optimistic perspective on life.

I think this is more hopeful than the message that came to me at the P.M.A. seminar. The seminar leaders taught us a lot about communication, understanding, time management, and human relations. But they left out God and assumed that human maturity comes only from human effort and positive thinking. Would somebody like to design a seminar on C.M.A. instead?

11

HOW TO HANDLE
shyness

I knew it was coming, but I still found it hard to believe. My college classmates were about to celebrate the twenty-fifth anniversary of our graduation.

A couple of days after the reunion invitation arrived, I dusted off our old yearbook and looked at the "graduating seniors." What a fine-looking group we were! (There can be no place for modesty on important occasions like this.) Wearing our finest clothes and postwar haircuts, each of us radiated self-confidence in the academic robe that added dignity to our senior portraits. Of course the photographer had only one robe, which we donned in turn for our appearance before the camera. But the yearbook gave the impression that we had just come from a ceremony bathed in splendor, dominated by the moment when we collected our diplomas accompanied by the strains of "Land of Hope and Glory"—that magnificent music written in praise of Britain but played at almost every graduation in North America.

In the quarter-century since our graduation, some of my classmates have become highly successful lawyers, doctors, professors, theologians, businessmen, educators, and politicians. I suspect others have seen their marriages fail, their careers collapse, their health deteriorate, or their hopes fade. Maybe some are facing middle-life crisis, even now, while others are at the peak of their creativity and influence. It

would be fun to see these people again, and I'm glad somebody is arranging a silver anniversary reunion.

But I don't think I'll be there!

I could say that the reunion is not at a convenient time,
or that it's too far away. It also is true that I don't want to
spend the money for the trip. Since my wife and I don't get
away as a couple very often, wouldn't it be better to vacation
at some place other than my old class reunion?

Deep within me, however, I think there is another reason
for avoiding social gatherings like this. I tend to be shy.

Some of my friends won't believe this. They know that I
can handle myself without blushing or getting tongue-tied in
social situations. I'm not opposed to meeting new people,
small-talk is no big problem (even though I don't enjoy it),
and I can speak without nervousness before a thousand people.

But I am reluctant to ask questions in a church business
meeting. I can teach graduate students with confidence, but
almost never muster the courage to make a statement in
faculty meetings or to comment in a Sunday school class.
Only once have I ever been called "shy," but at least sometimes that label is accurate.

I am not alone! A team of researchers from Stanford
University has been studying shyness for several years, and
their results are fascinating. A survey of several thousand
people revealed that over 80 percent labeled themselves
"shy," at least in some situations or at some time in life.
Shyness is of concern to people of all ages and is seen equally
in both women and men. Some well-known people who seem
to radiate self-confidence—Phyllis Diller, Lawrence Welk,
Elizabeth Taylor, Johnny Mathis, Barbara Walters, and Johnny Carson, to name a few—have all admitted in interviews
that they are shy. With refreshing honesty, comedienne Carol Burnett told the Stanford researchers that she has always
been shy. She said her ability to make people laugh began
during childhood when she "joked around with the kids and
clowned around just to get over the fear of not being liked,"
because she was "poor and not very pretty."

Even though it is common among both rich and poor, shyness is hard to define and not easy to change. Some people seem to like their shyness. It lets them be "reserved" or "unassuming," and they can enjoy life without the pressures of being noticed. More often, however, the shy person is anxious and uncomfortable. He or she holds back because of insecurity, fear of embarrassment, and a poor self-image. In addition, the Stanford researchers discovered that eighty-five percent of all shy people feel self-conscious—strongly preoccupied with themselves and with the reactions of other people.

All this would suggest that shyness is a tendency—sometimes mild, often strong—to pull away from others because we feel awkward, fearful, or insecure in their presence. According to psychologist Phillip Zimbardo, perhaps the world's greatest expert on this subject, the shy person is afraid of people, especially people who for some reason are emotionally threatening: strangers because of their novelty or uncertainty, authorities who wield power, members of the opposite sex who represent potential intimate encounters, or acquaintances who might criticize or reject us if we make a social blunder or say something stupid.

For some people, shyness is so strong and gripping that it can only be dislodged and overcome with the help of a professional counselor. Most of us, however, can rise above shyness on our own or with the help of a friend, especially if we understand and seek to apply some simple principles.

Decide to change. Have you ever noticed how much we are influenced by labels? A teacher, parent, or coach may tell us that we are "clumsy," "stupid," or "nervous," and, without giving it much further thought, we believe the labels and act as if they were true.

I wonder how often shyness starts with such a label? A child who is quiet, sensitive, self-conscious, lonely, or—like Carol Burnett—"poor and not very pretty," is often assumed to be shy. Since powerful adults believe this and state it clearly, the child accepts the "shyness" label and it sticks for life. Shyness, then, can become an excuse for withdrawing and not reaching out to people. We assume that shyness is inborn, when really it is a pinned-on label that we have meekly accepted without question.

It is probable that our society teaches people to be shy. In countries like China and Israel, shyness is not very common because children are made to feel special, are encouraged to express their ideas freely, and are not in competition with each other. In contrast, Germans, Japanese, Taiwanese, and Americans tend to be more shy, presumably because of an emphasis on competition and the need for approval.

Shortly after I started this article, my seventh-grade daughter rushed in to give a report of her entry in the junior-high science fair. "The judges were nice to me and I won a blue ribbon," she exclaimed, "but they weren't very nice to my friend David. They told him his project wasn't any good, even though he worked hard on it." According to my daughter, David isn't easily crushed by such criticism, but I wonder if he'll enter the contest next year? Some kids would pull back in response to such criticism and be labeled "shy," maybe even by their concerned and loving parents.

Whatever the reason for our reticence, we're not likely to change until we decide to be different. Those Stanford researchers discovered that shyness, even of the severest variety, has been and can be changed. To start, we must accept the idea that improvement is possible.

Work at overcoming fear. If shyness is really a fear of people and social situations, it would follow that to reduce shyness we must overcome our fears.

Most of us aren't shy when we are at home or when we are doing a job that we know well. Shyness more often comes when we are with people whom we don't know and in situations that are filled with uncertainty.

Think, for example, about how hard it is to apply for a job. The prospective employer is a stranger, and we are in a situation where we have no control. We fear that we might be embarrassed or rejected in the personnel office, and because of this fear, the little courage we had melts like ice on a warm day.

It can be helpful at such times to practice the job interview ahead of time. Think about how you will dress and what you will say. You might have to *imagine* yourself going to the office and asking for the interview before you bring yourself to walk up to the door in person.

Strange as it may seem, it sometimes helps to practice the interview with a friend who tries to act like a personnel manager. You might even pretend to be the interviewer. What would you look for in yourself? This is not reality, of course, but there is evidence to suggest that when people act with confidence and calmness they begin to feel more self-assured.

Everybody knows that young children are most often afraid when they are alone. It's the same with adults. We find it easier to attend a party, explore a new shopping center, start college, or visit a different church when someone else goes with us. (Job hunting is often harder because we have to do it by ourselves.) If you can find an understanding friend to help you conquer shyness, the battle will be easier.

As Christians, of course, we already have a friend who is with us at all times. The Bible says nothing about shyness, but it does talk about fear. We read that the perfect love of Christ "casts out" fear and gives us the confidence to go on. Prayer, therefore, is important if we hope to experience the divine help which enables us to overcome the fear of people and social situations.

Talk to yourself. Most of us go through life talking to ourselves. Usually we don't do this out loud, but silently we are constantly making plans, evaluating the world around us, and repeating messages about what we think we are like.

I wonder how often we create our own problems by telling ourselves things that aren't true. We don't always wait for other people to label us. Over and over again we tell ourselves "I'm no good, I'm a failure, I'm less capable than other people, I'll never succeed." These ideas undercut our own self-esteem, eat away our self-confidence, and increase our shyness.

Several years ago some psychologists proposed a deceptively simple technique called *thought stopping.* As soon as you become aware of a self-defeating thought, say "Stop." Say it out loud if nobody else is around. Then try to direct your attention to something else. At first the thoughts will come tumbling into your mind with increasing frequency, but before long they will be less common.

It also helps if you challenge your own thoughts. Who says you are shy? Have you really got good reasons to believe that you are stupid or incompetent? Maybe you've been concerning yourself with some things that aren't true.

Many psychologists believe that we also can counter self-destructive talk by trying to create a "positive mental attitude." For some people, this may work, but surely it is better to think more realistically. It's realistic to recognize that we have been created by God; we are individuals whom He loves with no strings attached. When we confess our sins and failures, He forgives. When we admit that Jesus Christ is God's son, He adopts us as His children and gives us special gifts and abilities that allow us to serve Him. We then have every reason to tell ourselves: "I'm not junk. I'm a child of the King. I can do all things with Christ who gives me strength."

That's realistic self-talk. It builds self-confidence and strengthens self-esteem. Research has shown that low self-esteem and shyness go together. When we begin to get a realistic picture of our self-worth as followers of Christ, our self-esteem goes up and shyness begins to fade. That's a message worth telling ourselves and others.

Reach out to others. At the end of her interview, Carol Burnett was asked if the experience with shyness had taught her anything that might be passed on to others.

"I tell my three daughters," she replied, "that other people have the same problems you have. I tell them not to be so selfish as to think the world revolves around what people think about you. They're not always evaluating and judging you in critical ways. They're thinking about themselves." You have to reach out to people because "when we touch another person . . . we are helping ourselves."

Sometimes I think many of us are too introspective and concerned about our own problems. The Bible seems to put a lot of emphasis on helping others, and it may be that there is no better way of handling shyness.

Do you remember those young people in China and Israel? They tended to be less shy because their parents and teachers gave encouragement and love. There were no "put downs" because somebody's science project wasn't perfect and there was little concern about who was best. Mutual caring removed shyness from the kids and probably from the parents as well.

Shyness is more likely to appear when we think we will be evaluated. When we reach out to help and encourage others their reactions and evaluations hardly concern us, and we feel less shy.

One of my favorite Bible figures is Barnabas. Little is known about him except that he had a reputation for encouraging people. I'd be willing to bet that Barnabas wasn't shy!

Maybe this also says something about that college reunion. It would be good to see my old classmates, and there isn't any need for me to be concerned about whether they evaluate me or how I size them up after twenty-five years. I might even be able to do a little encouraging there.

Perhaps I'm not too shy to go after all!

12

HOW TO HANDLE
a crisis

It was a warm sunny afternoon in Chicago. Cars were already heading out of town for a long holiday weekend. At O'Hare, one of the world's busiest commercial airports, hordes of travellers were moving back and forth through the corridors, creating the hectic scenes so characteristic of air terminals on Friday afternoons.

Suddenly a violent explosion rocked the area. A seething mass of flame and thick black smoke rolled into the sky and blotted out the afternoon sun. American Airlines Flight 191 disintegrated in a crash only a few seconds after takeoff. It was the worst air disaster in U.S. history. Almost three-hundred people died instantly, and in the hours that followed, friends and relatives around the world were jolted with the news of loved ones who suddenly were gone. Lost amid news reports of this horrible disaster was an equally grim statistic: More than five-hundred people had died on the ground—in highway fatalities and in other accidental deaths during the holiday weekend. Thousands of their relatives were plunged into grief.

Grief, like death, is a common experience, a crisis point in life. But grief is not the only crisis people encounter. Whenever some event or series of circumstances jolts us psychologically or interferes with our routines of daily living, we face a crisis. The experience is common today, just as it was in Bible times. Abraham, Isaac, Moses, Elijah, Job, Daniel, and a host of other Old Testament people encountered crises. Jesus faced crisis (especially at the time of His crucifixion), and so did the disciples, Paul, and many early believers.

Contemporary psychologists have divided crises into three types, each of which has both modern and biblical examples. First, there are *accidental crises* which come when there is a sudden threat or an unanticipated loss. The death (expected or sudden) of a loved one, the coming of a serious illness, the loss of one's possessions or status, the onset of war or economic depression—these are sudden stresses which affect us just as they influenced Job. Within a short period he lost his family, wealth, health, and status. His marriage appears to have been strained, and he reacted with confusion, anger, and inner turmoil—all of which are common crisis emotions.

The second type of crises, *developmental crises,* usually are anticipated, but they nevertheless can be difficult to accept. Adapting to a new job, adjusting to marriage or the birth of children, coping with middle age, changing vocations, moving, facing retirement or failing health, watching one's grown children leave home—each of these requires us to readjust and to find new ways of problem solving. In the Bible, Abraham and Sarah coped with moving, criticism, many years of childlessness, adjustment to parenthood late in life, and a variety of family stresses. These are turning points in life. Some are even anticipated eagerly, but they often involve pain and require wise decision making.

Third, there are "existential" or *life status crises*. These come when we are faced with disturbing truths about ourselves and our status in life. It is difficult, for example, to accept that "I'm a failure," "my life has no purpose," "my illness is incurable," "my marriage is falling apart," "I've got nothing to believe in," "I'm no longer employed," or "people don't like me because of the color of my skin." We can deny these thoughts for a while, but they keep coming to our attention and must be faced realistically.

Elijah once had an experience like this. After a great spiritual victory, he was chased by Queen Jezebel, ran into the wilderness, concluded that he was a useless failure, and prayed that God would take away his life. Such despair is a common reaction to crises.

In handling these crises we must begin by admitting that they are common life disruptions, experienced by everyone. They can immobilize us, but they can also help us to mature, depending on how they are handled.

Look, for example, at the accompanying questionnaire. This lists some common ways in which people deal with crises. As you read these questions you might want to think of a specific crisis in your life and circle true or false, depending on how you most often tend to react.

1. I try to deny problems when they arise.	T	F
2. I try to understand the situation more fully.	T	F
3. I try to hide my feelings of sorrow, anger, guilt, etc.	T	F
4. I try to talk about problems with friends, relatives or a pastor.	T	F
5. I try to find someone to blame for the crisis.	T	F
6. I usually assume that the crisis is punishment from God or that it means He is dissatisfied with me.	T	F
7. I try to pray about the situation.	T	F
8. I try to consider practical ways of coping with the problem.	T	F
9. I try not to think about the problem.	T	F
10. I try to avoid other people, so I can work on the problem myself.	T	F
11. I think the best way the handle a crisis is to do nothing until the problem resolves itself.	T	F
12. If I can, I try to help others, even when I am facing a crisis.	T	F

When crises arise, it is unhealthy to pretend that the problem does not exist, or to deny our feelings of confusion, hurt, disappointment, and anger. Some people try to ignore their crises, perhaps hoping they will disappear. Others evade the problem by plunging into work, busy activity, or excessive drinking. Still others blame God or other people for the crises of life and slide into a do-nothing attitude of depressed cynicicism and bitterness. Often there is a tendency to withdraw from other people, including those who could help us most. All these actions help us to avoid a crisis, but they don't help us to deal with it in a straightforward and helpful way.

In contrast, we can meet crises in healthy ways such as the following:

Face the crisis honestly. The first step in healing is to acknowledge that there is a problem which needs to be solved.

Be honest about your feelings. Most crises are accompanied by feelings of guilt, anxiety, hurt, anger, resentment, and discouragement. To pretend that these feelings do not exist only serves to prolong the crisis and to make life more miserable.

Draw closer to people who can help. Friends, relatives, a pastor, or fellow church members can all give encouragement and guidance when a crisis arises. We need these people and they, in turn, need us when crises come into their lives. This is the biblical principle of bearing one another's burdens (Gal. 6:2).

Try to understand the situation. It can be helpful to understand what is happening to you in times of crisis. Recognize that some things are unchangeable (like the death of a mate), but that other issues can be changed (like the failure to communicate in marriage). Often our understanding is clearer when we can talk over the situation with another person.

Consider practical ways of coping with the problem. Now that the crisis has occurred, what can you do to handle the problem?

What steps can you take (however small) to "pick up life" and go on living? What skills, abilities, or training do you have that might be useful in meeting the crisis? How can you change yourself and/or your environment? Answering these questions with specific practical responses can be immensely helpful.

Accept responsibility for coping. Blaming others for causing the problem, or expecting others to solve our problems, doesn't help very much. Even when the crisis seems to have come from situations beyond your control, think about the responsibilities that you might have for coping.

Pray about the matter. Share your feelings and confusion with God, asking Him to give you the peace, wisdom, and guidance that He has promised.

Ponder what God is like. He is sovereign, all-knowing, ever present, powerful, and concerned about us—even in times of crisis. The Bible gives little (if any) support for the idea that crises reflect God's disfavor or desire to punish.

Meditate on the Bible. This is God's Word to the human race. At crisis times many of us don't feel like reading the Bible (especially if we are mad at God), but this is a time when we at least should listen to what God says about Himself, about us, and about our needs.

Reach out to others. Counselors have often discovered that one of the best ways to help yourself is to help others. This lets you keep a realistic perspective on your problem, and it can prevent you from moping about your difficulties.

Crises are never easy, but they can be opportunities for growth, especially if they are handled well. If you completed the questionnaire, and answered *true* on items 2, 4, 7, 8, and 12, and marked the rest *false*, you have learned the basis for coping with crises. If you checked different answers, these can give you some indication of how you can change to cope more effectively with crises in the future.

It is difficult to understand why Flight 191 crashed, why those five-hundred people died violently on Memorial Day, or why each of us encounters crises in life. As Christians we do not always have understanding, but we do have hope. Our hope is based on the promises of a powerful loving God who sustains us in the present and assures us of something better in the future. Such hope enables us to avoid despair and gives us energy to handle crises realistically and effectively.

13

HOW TO HANDLE
decisions

Each New Year's Day I like to think about my friend Rob. I remember him at other times, too, but in early January I recall his unique approach to New Year's resolutions.

Rob is almost fifty now, grayish and comfortably middle-aged. Married and the father of three teenagers, he might be called moderately successful. He's not rich or famous, but Rob has a good steady job and is an active churchman. He's also a thinker.

I found that out when he told me about a day ten years ago when he was reading the Sunday paper. A new decade was beginning, and the newspapers were filled with interesting speculations about the future. Interviews with famous people, comments from the experts, and articles by journalists were predicting what might happen in government, business, the economy, international politics, ecology, and education. As he read, Rob was struck with a sobering thought.

"What might happen to me during the next decade," he wondered, "and what about my family? What would I like to see happen in our lives during the next ten years?" Rob concluded that the government, scientists, and industrialists had plans for the future. His Church had some goals and so did his business, but there were no specific plans and goals for his family.

Putting down the news, Rob reached for a sheet of paper

and wrote what the date would be in exactly ten years. Then he wrote down his name, the name of his wife, and each family member. Next to the names he wrote the age that each member would be ten years hence. Then alone, and later with his wife and children, he started jotting down personal and family goals for the coming decade.

As you might expect, the family listed some things that they would like to *have* in the coming decade, but they also noted what they would like to *be:* more patient, more mature, more understanding, better able to get along. Since a list like this can be extremely vague, the family started thinking of specific, practical things that each could do to reach their goals.

Because of their religious convictions, I'm sure the family must have asked, "What does God want us to do?" and, "How can we determine His leading?" They also might have wondered, in planning for the future, how one might handle the difficult issue of making wise decisions.

Many years ago I heard Elton Trueblood speak on decision making. His talk was titled "The agony of choice," and, although the speech has been long forgotten, I often have remembered the truth in that simple title. Making choices can be agonizing, especially when the decisions are important, the alternatives equally desirable (or undesirable), and the implications far-reaching. Picking out something to wear in the morning can be a relatively minor decision, but it is much more difficult to decide whether or not to get married, change jobs, retire, submit to surgery, or make a big investment. During the next decade, most of us will face major decisions like these. For some readers the decisions must be made very soon. For some the decisions will have to be made quickly and without much prior thought.

Probably most Christians believe that God can and does guide our decision making. In the Bible, we read how He led people by visions and special signs on occasion, but even in ancient times this was very rare. Even rarer were the times when God gave prophecies to one person, who then told another what to do, and there is no evidence that He ever led by "inner feelings." The reading of horoscopes or consulta-tion with fortune-tellers wold appear to be inconsistent with biblical teaching because soothsayers, occultists, and those who attempt to call up the dead are clearly condemned in the Bible (Lev. 19:26, 31; 20:6; Deut. 18:10–12).

How, then, do we establish priorities and make decisions that are consistent with divine leading? How do we find God's will? The answer cannot be stated in a never-fail formula, but there are some decision-making principles that can be helpful.

First, we must *want God's leading* in making decisions. Most of us have had the experience of thinking "I'll go where you want me to go, dear Lord; I'll do what you want me to do—provided that your will is consistent with my prior plans, desires, and expectations." Often what we really want is God's "rubber stamp" approval of our personal wishes. Our minds are made up before we come to God, and we are little inclined to change.

The Bible does not picture people coming to God for approval of their established plans. Instead, they came with a willingness to be led. How did they get this willingness? They prayed.

Most of us, by nature, are not inclined to want divine leading. We need, therefore, to pray regularly: "Lord, help me to be willing to do your will."

Second, realize that we can *expect God's leading* in making decisions. Sometimes we seem to think that God likes to play hide-and-seek, expecting us to do His will, but then keeping His plans hidden from everyone except those who are "lucky" or intelligent enough to unravel divine mysteries. How inconsistent this is with the inspired words of Scripture: "Trust in the Lord with all your heart, and lean not on your own understanding; in all your ways acknowledge Him, and He will direct your paths" (Prov. 3:5–6, KJV).

When we want God's leading, we can expect it. He rarely leads in dramatic ways, but He leads, nevertheless, even though we might not feel led. Often His guidance comes through our God-given brains. This brings us to our third principle.

We should *ponder God's leading* in making decisions. Ask yourself such basic questions as the following:

• Does the Bible say anything that might help my decision? (Be careful not to pull verses or phrases out of context.)

• If I have more than one alternative, can I list the pros and cons of each one on paper?

• What is the most logical thing to do?

• What are my abilities, gifts, interests, and training? Do these influence what I will do?

• After pondering the above, are there circumstances, personal experiences, and feelings that might help with my decision?

"In the end," writes Blaine Smith in a recent book on guidance, "knowing God's will boils down to making a rational decision."

Fourth, it is helpful to *discuss God's leading*. It can be confusing, of course, to talk with too many people, but often one or two sensitive, thoughtful, wise persons can give us their perspectives as we make decisions.

Eventually, however, we must *act on what we assume to be God's leading*. Books on decision making often include the old illustration about moving vehicles: It is easier to steer a car that is moving than one that is parked. Once we have prayerfully and carefully considered the alternatives before us, it is good to start moving in the direction that seems best. If we sincerely want and expect divine leading, we can trust that God will continue to guide us as we pursue a course of action.

But what if it seems later that we have made a mistake? Might I suggest that we try to foget it and push on without self-condemnation? I once moved my family halfway across the country to join the faculty of a school that soon collapsed. Did I make a mistake? Only God knows the answer to that question. If I erred in my decision to move, it could be helpful to ponder how such error could be avoided in the future, but it is also helpful to quit mulling over what is past and to direct attention to the making of wise decisions in the future.

This brings me back to my friend Rob. After listing their priorities and making decisions ten years ago, the family launched into the new decade. It was a period that included heartache, grief, serious illness, vocational turmoil, and personal stress. Nevertheless, Rob's family also reached many of their goals, and they developed a new sense of gratitude, purpose, and family pride. Each January, instead of randomly listing a collection of idealistic New Year's resolutions, the family members have now learned to set carefully selected goals and plans which they may or may not be able to accomplish during the year ahead. When they are faced with major decisions, they expect and seek God's leading.

This January I hope Rob and his family don't forget to list their goals for the next decade. In our home, I think we will follow their example.

14

HOW TO HANDLE
competition

I must confess that I was surprised at myself. It was a warm, sunny day in July, and for the first time my neighbor was trying out his new underground sprinkler system. Sparkling in the summer sun, the cascading droplets of water reflected a rainbow of colors as they fell to the parched ground below. I was not conscious of any feelings of jealousy, but I did wonder how our thirsty lawn could possibly compare to the green expanse which was sure to persist next door. Our old hose could never water the grass like my neighbor's automatic sprinkler system. Suddenly I became aware of an inner competition with my neighbor over something as insignificant as the color of our lawns.

Competition is like that! It isn't always rational, it creeps up on us without warning, and at times it can pervade our whole way of thinking. Everyone expects that athletes will strive to surpass others and train to win. But competition is not limited to sports. It characterizes the business world, it is basic to the military, it is at the core of politics, it is a way of life for students, and it even can dominate the home. Children who compete in school, music, and little league often bring their anxieties home where the tension persists and sometimes explodes—to the surprise of innocent siblings or busy mothers. Husbands, working wives, and other employed family members compete in society and sometimes find it difficult to tame their tensions when the workday is over. Few households are free of competition among brothers and sisters, and certainly many married couples find themselves competing with one another.

Competition is so common in our culture that it once was considered to be an inborn human instinct. We now know that it is learned, but it comes so early that few, if any, of us reach adulthood without that urge to win over others. At times we find ourselves competing with relatives, friends, fellow workers, church members, and neighbors with whom we compare our homes, our children, our successes, and even the quality of our lawns.

Competition isn't all bad, of course. It can motivate, keep us alert, give opportunity for people to discover their gifts and abilities, provide enjoyment, and add zest to activities that otherwise might be dull or unpleasant. Spurred on by competition, many people learn more, accomplish greater things, develop skills, and reach levels of success they otherwise might never achieve. Although some people seem to thrive on competition (and others do not), probably all of us have grown because of the competitive spirit that dominates our society and pervades our lives.

But competition can also destroy. Pro basketball's Bob Cousy called competition "the killer instinct," a devastating force that can spread like cancer, compelling people to drive themselves unmercifully, to subject themselves to sustained and severe pressure, and to act unscrupulously in order to win. Competition is able to divide us, drain away our peace of mind, and wear us down physically.

Several years ago, for example, two San Francisco cardiologists wrote a thought-provoking and widely acclaimed book titled *Type A Behavior and Your Heart*. Type A people, the book suggested, are aggressive, impatient, work-dominated individuals who have "deep-seated insecurity," a lot of hidden anger, and (this is important) an excessive competitive drive. Sometimes these people work too much, drink too much, eat too much, and relax too little. They are the people most prone to heart attacks. For them, competition can lead to physical collapse.

The destructive effect of competition has been described even more dramatically by a psychiatrist who wrote about patients who are always running to succeed, but who rarely are satisfied. Afraid to slow down, they push on in a never-ending chase "engaged in a Marathon race, their eager faces distorted by strain, their eyes focused not upon their goal, but upon each other with a mixture of hate, envy, and admiration." This description might be slightly overdrawn, but it dramatically shows the harmful power of competition.

If the competitive drive existed only in the athletic world, many of us could overlook it, but competition affects all of us, and its destructive power is impossible to ignore. It is important, therefore, to develop what someone has called a "competition tolerance," an ability to live with competition and to help others do the same, without giving in to its smothering power. There are several ways in which this might be done.

Commit it to God. This is not a simplistic easy answer. It is a realistic starting point whereby we ask God to help us face the competition that is a fact of life in our society.

In the Old Testament, Jacob was a man whose life was dominated by competition. As a young man Jacob competed with his older brother, and because of his drive to win he was forced to leave home and flee to the household of his uncle. There Jacob married two sisters who competed with each other, and he appeared to be in constant competition with the uncle and his sons. Only in later life did he yield to God and cease the striving that had created so many problems in his life.

Psychologist Robert Goldenson has written that "there is no more complex question in the field of psychology than that of competition." Surely, then, we need to seek God's constant wisdom as we face this issue in ourselves and others.

Reduce competition in the home. I have a student who coaches the local "midget" hockey team. "The kids are fun to work with," my friend stated recently, "but some of the parents are impossible. They pressure the young players to succeed and heap scorn and criticism upon any son who does not do well." These parents are teaching type A behavior to their children and are putting them under tremendous pressure to compete and win.

Surely the home should not harbor such attitudes. Instead, it should be a haven from the pressure-cooker competition of our culture. When children constantly are pushed to succeed, compared unfavorably with others, urged to compete, and criticized for failure, a competitive atmosphere pervades the family. As every parent is aware, no two children have the same abilities, interests, or personalities, even when they grow up in the same home. In our house, therefore, we try not to contrast report cards, musical skills, or athletic abilities. We don't always succeed, of course, but we attempt to emphasize the individual abilities of each person and to resist making comparisons between the children. Although they make comparisons among themselves, we try to emphasize each person's unique gifts, helping family members to accept and realistically evaluate their unique strengths and weaknesses.

This applies to adults as well as children. Tension is increased when critical comments between husband and wife are intended to "put down" each other and when one's mate is compared unfavorably to relatives or friends. In such an atmosphere, family members learn to compete at home, and such a home provides no haven from the competitive pressures of society.

Separate competition from the self-concept. Very often we determine our worth in terms of how well we succeed in competition with others. People who fail quickly get the idea that they are "no good," and this brings feelings of inferiority sometimes accompanied by bitterness, withdrawal, negativism, a tendency to criticize, self-pity, and at times futile attempts to keep on trying to win. Sometimes parents attempt to boost their sagging egos by pushing their children to accomplish what the parents failed to achieve themselves. This creates tension for everyone.

Frequently we should remind ourselves and each other that every person is loved by God. He created us, sent His son to die for us, adopted believers as His children, and gives each of us gifts and abilities. In God's sight we are all valuable, even when we fail. The Creator is not concerned about our looks, intellect, strength, status, or ability to win a competition with someone else. He wants us to run the race of life and to win not by beating out others, but by serving Christ with the abilities and gifts we have been given. Perhaps one of the saddest commentaries on the church today is that we Christians have fallen into a mind-set which emphasizes cut-throat competition and equates self-worth with winning the status, power, and money that others do not possess. We have forgotten that God made each of us unique and gave us gifts, responsibilities, and opportunities that are important to Him, even though they may not be valued by the society around us.

Rethink our view of success. Recently I was invited to give a series of lectures at a college in another part of the country. As I rode to the campus from the airport, my host described the speakers who had come in previous years. "They were brilliant speakers," I was informed, "capable, informed, and outstanding in their ability to communicate." As this conversation continued, I felt less and less adequate. Surely I could never live up to the standards of those who had come before, and I began to ponder how it would be possible to get back to the airport and flee home. It was important for me to be successful as a visiting lecturer on that campus, but I was so busy comparing myself to others that I had forgotten my own uniqueness and God-given strengths.

Later, as I waited to be introduced, I began to see my task in a new perspective. "I am here to do the best I can," I told myself. "I have prepared carefully and even if I fail, the world will not end; God and my family will still love me, and life will go on." Quickly I relaxed and was able to give my speeches without worrying about whether or not these talks were better or worse than those who had preceded me.

Have you ever noticed how much we compete with others in our minds? So often we compare ourselves to someone who appears to be a better parent, a more capable hostess, a more charming personality, a more dedicated Christian, or superior in our field of work. Rarely do we realize that these people who seem so capable probably are insecure and also might be competing mentally as well— perhaps even with us.

The apostle Paul once discovered that the Christians in Corinth had divided into denominational factions and were competing with each other in an attitude of jealousy and strife. These attitudes concerned Paul, but he appeared to have no concern about who was the most successful Christian leader. "What difference does it make?" he asked. We are all God's servants, each with unique abilities, working as a team, and not trying to compete with one another.

In an age when people appear to be driven by the need to succeed and by a desire to win over others, we need to remember the words of Jesus. To really be successful in God's eyes, he told his disciples, we should be servants, helping and encouraging one another instead of competing.

Compete against ourselves, not against others. This, of course, is difficult to do in practice, but it reduces tension and makes life a lot more pleasant.

When my wife and I entertain, we find that our dinner parties often are followed by a late-night "postmortem" while we do the dishes together. We discuss the guest list, the food, the table setting, and other details of the evening—not in an effort to compare ourselves to others, but in a desire to determine how we can do better next time. We compete against our own past record, pleased when we make progress, and especially analytical when we are less successful.

This attitude of competing against ourselves can enter every aspect of our lives. I hope this book will be better than the last one I wrote, but not as good as the next one. I want my spiritual life to be better now than it was last year, and even better next year. As each new year dawns I want to be a better husband and father than I was the year before. Such an attitude motivates me. It also prevents the bitterness and destructive "putdowns" that can come when I spend time comparing myself to others and worrying about winning.

Learn the value of cooperation. The Bible is a book that emphasizes mutual caring, burden-bearing, and support. Within its pages we are instructed to help one another, not in a spirit of competition, but in an attitude of teamwork and cooperation.

In this age of competition, teamwork is not easy. Most of us have to work constantly at developing our competition tolerance. We have to resist the pressures to win over others in a spirit of intolerance of insensitivity. The place to start counteracting competition is with prayer and with an evaluation of our own attitudes and values.

I'm even learning to develop these attitudes with my neighbor. I still don't have an underground sprinkler system, and probably never will. At times his grass is greener than mine, but we work together on our lawns, share responsibility in caring for a little piece of village property, and exchange pleasant comments as we work alongside each other during the warm months of summer. This is more healthy, and more biblical, than constantly competing. It doesn't make my grass greener, but it makes life a lot more pleasant.

15

HOW TO HANDLE
criticism

When it happened, several years ago, I found it annoying and ridiculous. Now, when I think about it, the whole thing seems incredible, almost crazy.

I had finished my courses in graduate school and had moved to the West Coast where I was to begin a program of practical training in counseling. The work was rigorous but there still was time for church, and soon I found myself involved in the active college and career group of a large congregation. Before long I was elected president of the group and watched with real satisfaction as our numbers grew and our outreach expanded.

Then it happened! I was told "confidentially" that some established members of the church had concluded that I was a communist agent, sent from the Midwest to attract a following of Christian young people who would rise up against their country when it came time for "the revolution." The fact that I had grown up in Canada made me even more suspect. In the opinion of my critics (who never confronted me directly), I was not just a dangerous revolutionary masquerading as a Christian. I was a foreign spy!

I was dumbfounded! Nothing could have been further from the truth, and it was amazing that my vigorous church activities could have been so misinterpreted. When I went to the pastor and offered to leave, he smiled kindly and admitted that he had heard from the critics.

"Forget what they think," he advised. "Keep on doing what you believe God wants you to do."

Then he added a comment which I have never forgotten. "Whenever you are trying to do something worthwhile you can expect to be criticized—often unjustly."

The Bible would support this conclusion. In both the Old and New Testaments, people were criticized, sometimes unfairly. Jesus, for example, was called a glutton, a drunkard, a friend of sinners (Matt. 11:19), and even a colleague of the devil (Matt. 12:24). On several occasions He was accused of breaking religious laws, and when He went to weep at the grave of Lazarus some of the neighbors complained because Jesus hadn't come soon enough to prevent His friend from dying. On one occasion the Lord almost seemed to throw up His hands in despair and proclaim that there was no way to avoid criticism (Matt. 11:18–19).

Sooner or later, most of us make this discovery. We learn, too, that almost nobody likes criticism, not even the kind that is supposed to be constructive. There are several reasons for this.

First, *criticism hurts,* especially when the criticism isn't based on accurate information. It really bothered me to have those church members believing and spreading false rumors. Their criticism was not based in fact, and they lacked the courtesy of identifying themselves and checking out their conclusions with me.

I enjoy reading the memoirs of political leaders, and have been impressed by how often these people feel that they have been criticized unjustly by those who lack correct information. Recently there appeared a cartoon in which two little kids were discussing presidential elections. "I wouldn't want to be elected President," one boy exclaimed. "I get blamed for enough things as it is!" Probably every public figure feels like that, at times, and so do those of us who are ordinary citizens. It isn't pleasant to be criticized.

Why, then, don't we just ignore the criticism and not let it bother us? For most of us this is difficult, if not impossible, because *criticism attacks our self-esteem.* It implies that we are unimportant, deceptive, wrong, or worthless, and our critics often use just enough accurate information to make their charges plausible. Soon we begin to wonder if the critic might at least be partially right, and this begins to erode our self-confidence.

Psychologist Archibald Hart has described a housewife who was criticized by her husband every time she cooked an imperfect meal. Before long, she forgot all those times in which she had prepared a good meal. To herself, she began to think, "although I succeed most of the time, I do make mistakes periodically, so I guess my husband is right. I'm a failure as a cook." The husband's criticism was based on some facts. She did fail at times. But the criticism overlooked the many successes, and the housewife was bothered because of the implication that she was inadequate as a homemaker and perhaps as a wife.

Sometimes, such *criticism reminds us of an unpleasant past.* People who constantly were criticized as children often become adults who are supersensitive to the opinions of others. The criticized child feels helpless and "put down." When he or she reaches adulthood, it is difficult to shake off these feelings. New criticism reminds us of the past and continually opens up old wounds which we would prefer to have heal and disappear.

But it isn't always possible to wipe out the past, and this brings us to another reason why we don't like to be criticized: *criticism often leaves us defenseless.* Not long ago, a book appeared in which the author criticized me, using such words as "deplorable" and "ignorant" to describe my work. As you might expect, this attack left me angry, but I also felt helpless. How could I defend myself? How could I correct the writer's conclusions which, from my perspective, were wrong? How could I present my side of the issue to the book readers, or to a writer who was unavailable and apparently unwilling to budge from his published evaluation of me?

Most of us feel a sense of frustration and helplessness when we are criticized. We may want to defend ourselves or to express our point of view, but it isn't easy to put our thoughts into words, and sometimes we don't even know our critics. As a result, we feel that someone has dumped garbage on us, and there is very little we can do to avoid the stench.

But there *are* things we can do. We can handle criticism by admitting that it exists, acknowledging that it hurts, then asking ourselves some questions that will help us rise above the barbs of our critics.

Who is criticizing me? Strange as it may seem, the answer to this question may be "nobody." We may assume that someone else is being critical, but when we stop to think about it, we realize that the criticism really is all in our own minds, a figment of our imaginations. It doesn't make sense to get upset about criticism that doesn't even exist.

At other times, of course, the criticism is real, but the critics are not very credible. Sometimes critics lack accurate information, so their opinions are not based on facts. At other times, the critics are expressing their own anger, frustration, and prejudice rather than giving a considered evaluation of our actions or work.

Many years ago I concluded that book reviews often say more about the reviewer than about the book. Some critics are never pleased with anything. To be critical is a part of their personalities, and we only frustrate ourselves when we try to keep such people happy. When criticism comes from those who lack accurate knowledge or a gentle attitude, it is best not to take the criticism too seriously.

This does not hide the fact, however, that some critics are important. They do have valid information, and their criticisms are worth considering. Even if the criticism seems unfair, it can't be ignored when it comes from one's employer or family. Think of that homemaker, for example. It would be difficult for her to ignore her husband's complaints, even though they may not be fair. This brings us to a second question.

Why is someone criticizing me? This is not easy to answer, because it means that we must try to understand the motives of our critics. People criticize for a number of reasons, including the following:

• They see something wrong or incomplete, and they sincerely want to offer suggestions for improvement.

• They are insecure people who are always finding fault with others. Such people try to build up themselves by knocking down everyone else.

• They are angry, bitter people who never see anything positive and appear to take delight in constant fault finding.

• They are pressured people—individuals whose patience is wearing thin because they are under stress at work, home, or elsewhere. Because they are pressured and impatient, such people cannot tolerate imperfection or ineffeciency, so they tend to explode in criticism. Sometimes highly critical remarks even burst forth from the lips of our children who are expressing frustration and may not be nearly as critical as they sound.

• They are people with very high standards for others and sometimes for themselves. Such people are critical of those whose standards and performances are less than perfect.

From this list we can conclude that criticism often arises as much from the critic's own personality and stresses as from the things being criticized. I try to remember this, especially when I am inclined to criticize my children. Sometimes their actions are not really as bad as I imply, but I find myself criticizing because of my own tension or impatience.

Is there truth in the criticisms of me? When we are criticized, our most immediate response is to feel threatened and get angry. Before overreacting, however, it is helpful to ask if the critic is right.

Not long ago, a young man approached me following a talk that I had given to some college students. "Your talk was interesting," he stated, "but I think your ideas are irrelevant and unrealistic."

As he continued talking, I could feel my muscles tense. His criticism was an attack on my self-esteem as well as on my ideas. I was uncomfortable and uncertain how to respond, but I recognized that some of his observations were accurate. When I admitted this and decided not to be defensive, we had a lively and helpful discussion.

If we can get over our initial feeings of threat and anger, we can learn from our critics. We need not assume that they are always right, but neither are they always wrong. As we ponder their criticisms, we must seek to find out whether the criticisms are based on facts, then decide if the criticism is worth heeding.

How should I respond to criticisms of me? There are several answers to this question.

First, we can discuss the criticism. Because of our emotional involvement, it can be difficult to evaluate criticism by ourselves. At such times it can be beneficial to discuss the issues with a friend who can help us get a clearer perspective on what the critics are saying. There can also be value in discussing the criticism directly with our critics. If you feel the criticism is unjust, say so. Try to listen and present your point of view in an atmosphere of respect for the other person's opinions, with a willingness to avoid confrontation and self-defensiveness.

Second, we can evaluate the criticism. This has been implied in the previous paragraphs. Most criticism has elements of truth that can be helpful and parts that can be ignored or discounted, especially when we feel that the critic is to be discounted.

Let us return one more time to that homemaker. She needs to recognize that, although she fails at times, such failures are common. No one is perfect (including her husband), and in spite of her failures she also succeeds frequently, at home and probably elsewhere.

This should be remembered.

It has been suggested that when we are criticized, most of the damage comes because we let the criticisms fester in our minds, we magnify them out of porportion, focus on the negative, and fail to see the positive side of our lives. Carried away by this introspection, we become hypersensitive to criticism, defensive, and sometimes immobilized or afraid to act, lest we be criticized again.

This brings us to a third way of responding to criticism. We can grow from it. Although criticism can be devastating, it also can be helpful. It can point out weaknesses and alert us to things in our lives that should be changed and improved. Even when we have been angered by a critic or prevented from responding, criticism forces us to think more clearly about our actions. As a result, we may change when this seems wise, or we may conclude with greater clarity that we shouldn't change, in spite of the criticism.

Throughout all this it is helpful to maintain a sense of humor, important to do the best we can, and crucial that we do what we think is right before God. Criticism is a part of life, but criticism can be handled. That's what my pastor told me back in those post college days, and since that time I've never had to worry about any more talk of my being a subversive agent.

16

HOW TO HANDLE
hostility

Almost everyone, I suppose, knows that psychologists were the first people to come up with the idea of psychological tests. We have invented a whole host of ingenious devices—questionnaires, ink blots, puzzles, or fill-in-the-blank forms, to name a few—which are supposed to reveal the hidden truth about the test-taker's intelligence, personality, aptitudes, abilities, or interests. Although some of these tests aren't very accurate (you've probably suspected that), many *do* give useful information that can be helpful as we learn more about ourselves and make plans for the future.

Not long ago, I was thinking about this while driving my kids to school. "Is it possible," I wondered out loud, "that the best test of personality comes not from a psychologist's ingenuity, but by watching what people do behind the wheel of a car?" Such an idea isn't very novel or scientific, but it sure raises some interesting questions in my mind.

Why, for example, do otherwise law-abiding citizens break the speed limit, fudge on the rules of the road, and delight in trying to avoid the uniformed people who lurk in hidden places with those sneaky radar detectors?

Why do some of us who normally are caring, considerate pillars of nonviolence, turn into aggressive, hot-tempered competitors in the five o'clock traffic jam (which, with undying optimism, we still like to call the evening "rush")?

Why do some generally patient individuals seethe with impatient annoyance when they get into the driver's seat?

Why are there motorists who like to blow their horns, shake their fists, dart in and out of traffic, or refuse to let others into a line? Why do some drivers dawdle along, seemingly oblivious to everyone else and not inclined to budge, especially in response to the horn-honking or headlight-flashing from other cars?

Why, I wonder, do other drivers frequently give the right-of-way to fellow motorists, or stop to help when a disabled vehicle and its driver are stranded alone at the side of the road where everyone else is whizzing by?

As a psychologist, I know of one thing that we do better than designing tests: we are experts in asking hard questions. Finding answers isn't as easy!

Perhaps driving has something to do with our urge to compete, our impatience, or our self-centered thinking. Probably some motorists are reacting out of fear, especially those of us who drive regularly on big-city freeways. Maybe many people feel safe enough and free enough to let their real personalities spill out whenever they are enclosed within those powerful moving steel boxes that we call cars. Buoyed by a sense of power or control, some drivers react to strangers in ways that would never even be considered at home, at work, at church, or at any other place where they are known.

The experts on driver behavior might have some other explanations, but I also wonder if a lot of motorist behavior can be summed up in one word: *hostility.*

Hostility is a gnawing sense of inner anger, a response to some frustration that has persisted for a long period of time. Hostile people may hide their anger and sometimes don't even see it in themselves. On the surface there can be a calm friendliness, but inside there is a brewing caldron of resentment that seeps out subtly or sometimes explodes like a spewing volcano.

Hostility can be common. If it was limited to a few impatient and angry drivers, most of us wouldn't think further about hostility. But the problem is much broader. Certainly some people tend to be more hostile than others, and there are differences in the human ability to hide emotions. Nevertheless, many of us would agree with the man who wrote that "no one can be constantly and totally free of hostility." It is "the chief saboteur of the mind," wrecking interpersonal relations, tearing up families, contributing to disease, and bringing about misery, discouragement, inefficiency, hurt feelings, and accidents—sometimes on the highways.

Hostility can be well hidden. I know a man who is a powerful preacher and a respected pastor. In social situations he is charming and well known for his sense of humor. His jokes often put down other people, however. His sermons contain cutting comments and there are brief but intense flashes of anger in some of his statements at business meetings. Unlike the anger of Jesus, which always was directed against sin and against those who practiced it, my friend's anger appears to be a self-centered, bitter resentment over personal injustices. We've never talked about this, but I suspect that pastor is a basically hostile man whose hostility may not be noticed by many of his parishioners.

A conference speaker once remarked that "behind almost every successful man there is a hostile wife." Instead of resisting this idea, the audience of Christian leaders seemed to agree. Many women (and children) feel pushed aside while the husband builds his career, and sometimes his ministry, at the expense of time and attention given to the family. With increasing frequency, women too are building careers and giving their families second place. In such families, a resentful bitterness slowly builds up and begins to weaken the marriage. This happens even while everyone is smiling and problems are never admitted or even recognized.

Like termites who slowly eat away and destroy the foundations of a house, hostility subtly cripples relationships and undermines our emotional, physical, and spiritual well-being. It isn't surprising that the biblical writer warned against letting bitterness take root. "It springs up," he wrote, and "it causes deep trouble, hurting many in their spiritual lives" (Heb. 12:15, LB).

Hostility can be understood. Hostility usually "springs up" when we feel hindered in some way, deprived of something, or made to feel inferior. Children, for example, often develop hostility when parents show a lack of love, favoritism to another child, harsh and rigid discipline, excessive criticism, or a lack of respect. People who are part of a racial or other minority group may respond with hostility when there is unfair treatment, denial of opportunities, or the use of derogatory "put down" names.

If the hostility persists, it can influence us in a variety of ways. Some of these you might even see in yourself:

• Hostility can make us feel anxious and fearful. Whenever we sense that something is building up inside, we begin to feel uncomfrotable; we fear that we might lose control and say or do something that will be regretted later.

• Hostility can cloud our thinking. In response to any strong emotion, one's concentration, memory, judgment, and logic can be impaired. Sometimes, therefore, it is difficult to reason with hostile people, just as it is hard for others to talk to us when we are gripped by hostility.

• Hostility can lead to gullibility. Psychologists clearly have shown that we usually see what we want or expect to see. Do you remember President Nixon's famous "enemies list"? I suspect that White House personnel believed a lot of untrue things about the "enemies" because hostility had made it impossible for a more balanced viewpoint to prevail.

• Hostility can give rise to self-centered superiority. The more hostile we become, the more we are convinced that "I am right. The other guy is wrong!" In extreme cases, the hostile person never admits to making mistakes, refuses to cooperate, perpetually blames others, and slips into a self-centered way of thinking. All this hides the miserable feelings of inferiority and gives the hostile person some presumed reasons for being angry.

It probably won't surprise you to know that hostile

people often are lonely, suspicious, irritable, bitter, guilt-ridden, and sometimes "mad at the whole world." To hide these attitudes (often from themselves), these people may deny vehemently that they are hostile, or they may go to the opposite extreme and become overly friendly toward the person who is disliked. As resentment builds up inside, however, the body may begin to collapse under the stress. Insomnia, fatigue, ulcers, headaches, high blood pressure, or a variety of other illnesses may result.

When hostility comes to the surface, it is not because some driver is "cut off" on the freeway. It comes when people are hurt. The hurt and frustration give rise to anger, and if we are unable or unwilling to admit and express the anger, it stays hidden inside where it rots away like decaying garbage. For a while it can be neglected, but eventually the stench and clutter get too strong and something must be done to clean out the source of the problem.

Hostility can be handled. Dr. Milton Layden, an expert on hostility, has written that some popular methods for controlling resentments simply do not work. People who are caught in the hostility trap rarely change when they are told to:

Control your temper!
Look on bright side of things and think positively!
Take it easy, relax, and let bygones be bygones!
Keep busy so you don't have time to get angry!
Put on a happy face!
Use your sense of humor!
Vent your emotions and clear the air!

Other people don't like to hear such appeals, and they are almost impossible to apply to ourselves. Even if we could abide by the wisdom of these statements, they don't get to the root of the problem. We cope with hostility, not by reciting slogans, but by attacking the basic causes of our anger.

Begin by admitting that you are hostile. If other people

have noticed hostility in you, don't reject their opinion too quickly. They may see something real that your mind is trying to deny.

Second, although resentment and bitterness are harmful, remember that anger often is all right. Jesus got angry, and His Father has been described as a God of wrath. In itself, therefore, anger is not sinful. It becomes destructive when it is denied, uncontrolled, selfish, or allowed to develop into seething bitterness.

Third, it is helpful to remind ourselves that hostility often comes when we feel inferior and lacking in self-respect. Has something made you feel inferior? Even when you experience God's loving forgiveness and unconditional acceptance, it takes a long time to recognize that you are a worthy child of the king. If hostility has become a way of life, there may be value in talking with a friend or counselor about your self-image problems. Otherwise you may keep feeling inferior or worthless and perpetually angry because of your lack of self-respect.

It also is helpful to ask God to enable you to get rid of cynical attitudes. I have some friends who take delight in criticizing almost everything and everyone. It is easy to get caught up in their hostility game, especially when this involves gossip, criticism, or joking at someone else's expense. To avoid this, I have decided that it is best to limit my contacts with these hostile people. I try both to ignore their criticisms of others and to resist the tendency to get involved in their joking. When I'm alone, I resist the temptation to think unkind thoughts about people.

Psychologists sometimes talk about *collecting grievances*—making mental lists of what is wrong with someone else so we can dump all our complaints on the victim when we get a chance to assert our superiority. This habit soon gets us into a "mad" mind-set which isn't easy to shake. Such thinking doesn't help anyone, and it adds fuel to the fires of hostility. This brings us to one final conclusion.

Hostility can be resisted. Recently I saw a book that discussed ways to help others overcome their hostility. The suggestions were interesting: Don't argue with the hostile person; don't belittle or cast blame; be considerate and encouraging; build up the other person's self-respect; determine to be humble.

The writer of these suggestions gave no evidence of being a Christian, but his formula reminded me of an important Old Testament teaching: A soft answer turns away wrath (Prov. 15:1, LB).

To argue with a hostile person only increases his or her hostility. Much more effective is an approach that quietly builds up, encourages, and shows respect to others. When people feel respected, they are more likely to cooperate and can discuss issues in a less angry way.

This doesn't always work, of course! Some people wallow in their anger. They don't realize that they are so hostile, or they are unwilling to consider casting off their bitterness. In time, however, even many of these people have been known to budge in response to consistent and loving kindness.

The principle applies even on the highway. The next time your fellow drivers cut in front of you or blow the horn, don't bother to fight back. Tell yourself that it is their impatience and self-centered anger that is the problem, not yours. Recognize that their hostile impatience eventually can wear down their bodies and hasten their time of death. In contrast, you can determine to be more patient. Without closing your eyes, you might even pray for your fellow drivers.

That's a lot better than shaking your fist or leaning on the horn.

17

HOW TO HANDLE
success

Some people are fascinated by bookstores. While others are hooked on baseball, backgammon, or more serious pursuits, people like me prefer to wander past shelves of new volumes, perusing the titles and skimming the splashy covers.

The most interesting bookstore I can remember was a massive place which I visited frequently during my days as a student in England. It wasn't spacious and brightly lit, with attractively displayed merchandise neatly arranged by topic and sorted in alphabetical order. In contrast, the store seemed to be more like a string of old three-story houses, joined together by doors which had been knocked between the walls. There were steep and narrow staircases with steps that squeaked. The bare wooden floors sagged in spots, the lights were dim, and I seem to remember a lot of dust. But I loved the place! It provided the almost endless enjoyment of discovering old volumes and finding new titles.

In those student days, I reached the conclusion that book titles often give a good indication of the current interests and values of a society. Consider, for example, some of the books that have captured public attention in recent years. Many of them are "how to do it" books dealing in some way or another with the drive for success. This seems to have become an almost universal preoccupation with people, especially those of us who live in the United States or Canada. With blatant enthusiasm, recent books have told us how to acquire and use power, how to "get the upper hand," how to "pull your own strings," and how to "make a habit of success." One writer has published a "success system that never fails," one wants to "see you at the top," and another promises that "success can be yours."

Perhaps the most influential volume in this area is Michael Korda's best seller entitled *Success*. For almost three hundred pages the author tells us how to sit, stand, speak, act, and dress if we want to be successful. At the beginning of the book, he also instructs us how to think. We should tell ourselves, Korda suggests, that it is O.K. to be ambitious, greedy, and concerned about Number One. We should expect some tough infighting during our climb upward and should not feel guilty about "what is a perfectly natural and healthy ambition"—our right to succeed.

In various forms, such advice is repeated in dozens of books and articles, some written by Christians and most, I suspect, written by well-meaning authors who really do want to help their readers get ahead. The message is almost always the same:

You can be successful.

You can get what you want.

There are things you can do to succeed in life.

It probably is true that most of us want to succeed, and this desire isn't necessarily wrong. Children want to be successful in growing up and getting along with others. Teenagers want to be successful in dating, in peer relationships, in athletics, and (sometimes) in school work. Adults often strive for success in careers, marriages, handling finances, and the raising of children. Hopefully, most believers want to be successful in their Christian lives.

But what does it really mean to be successful? How do we live with success when and if it comes? If we don't succeed as we had hoped, how do we handle failure? These questions are not answered easily—especially in our society where we are so success-conscious that the fear of failure can be immobilizing, the experience of failure can be devastating, and the drive to succeed can be overwhelming. We are reluctant to admit failure, and we discover that part of the pain that comes with midlife results from the realization, "I have not succeeded as I had hoped. I probably will not reach all my life goals as I had planned."

In handling our concerns about success, may I suggest that the place to start is not with the success books, valuable though some of them may be. The place to begin is with our own attitudes. It can be helpful, for example, to ponder the following observations.

Most of us are ingrained with society's definition of success. Recently I heard about a student who asked his Christian college professor what it meant to be successful. "Don't worry about idealistic things like compassion, caring, and service," the professor replied. "As a Christian, you should seek to get status, money, power, and independence so the world can see that Christians can be successful like anyone else."

Without much deliberation, most of us have accepted this contemporary viewpoint: To be successful is to have prestige, personal resources, and power. When these conclusions become part of us, we look for excuses to fit them into our Christian perspective. We decide (sometimes with good reason) that power and money will enable us to worship God better, to give more, and to have a greater witness for Christ. Then we push to get ahead.

Our feelings of self-worth are tied to our level of success. When we meet a stranger, one of the first questions we ask is: "What is your work?" Quickly we evaluate others on the basis of occupation. The professional, the business person, or the community leader must be important, we conclude, because these persons are so obviously successful. But what about you or me? What if we are not successful in our occupations, marriages, or personal lives? It is easy to conclude, falsely, "Because I am not clearly successful, I must not be an important or worthwhile person." How easy it is to believe that our value as people is measured by our earthly success. How quickly we forget that God accepts and values us whether or not the world acclaims us as being successful.

Many people can never be successful according to the world's definition. Surveys of high-school students have shown that over half want to enter some profession. Most, of course, will not do so. A recent *Psychology Today* article reported that most people consider themselves to be better than average, but this, of course, is impossible. In spite of our hopes and aspirations, not many people become rich, powerful, or influential. There is limited room at the top, and few attain their dreams for success.

The Bible's view of success differs from the views of society. Do you remember the time when James and John came with their mother asking for a position of prominence in Christ's kingdom? Like many today, apparently these people assumed that power and status indicate success. Jesus agreed that this is the viewpoint of nonbelievers but taught that "it is not so" among followers of Christ. In what has been described as one of the most revealing passages in the New Testament, Jesus gave a divine formula for success: Whoever wants to be great should be a servant; whoever wants to be first should become a slave (Matt. 20:20–27).

Ours has been called the "me-generation," a time in history when people have learned to look to their own interests with little concern about others. We emphasize self-fulfillment, self-realization, and self-satisfaction. In the self-help books and elsewhere, little is said about self-sacrifice, self-discipline, giving, caring, or compassion.

One of my Christian friends recently argued that it is both unrealistic and idealistic to be a servant today. "We each must take care of ourselves," he stated. "We must push for personal success. The alternative is to be squashed in the competition." Such a view is not very spiritual, perhaps, but many would argue that it is the most realistic and most prevalent in our period of history.

But where does this leave the Christian who wants to be both successful and a sincere follower of Jesus Christ? It is encouraging to ponder one more conclusion about success and failure.

From God's perspective, everyone can be successful. Hebrews 11 gives a listing of people whom God considered to be successful. Some were very rich; others were poor. Many were famous, but a large number were unknown. Some were healthy; others were sick. While some lived to an advanced age, there were many who died early and sometimes violently. Nevertheless, these people were all men and women of faith whose success was measured in accordance with divine standards. Each was obedient to God, and apparently each had a servant attitude.

Some people, it seems, have the extra discipline, enthusiasm, strength, ability, and/or determination that enables them to attain success in accordance with the world's standards. Some have special education and opportunities which enable them to get ahead. If you are in this category, then thank God. Humbly recognize that it is He who has given you the interests, capabilities, motivation, and experiences which have enabled you to be successful. Don't be like the famous woodpecker whose peck on a tree came at the same instant as lightning struck. When the giant timber fell to the ground, the proud little bird exclaimed, "Look what I did. How great I am!" The truly successful person is humble, grateful to God, and not inclined to gloat over his or her status, power, prestige, and other marks of success.

Not long ago I spoke about this on a college campus and was approached by three students who were not impressed with my speech. "You implied that there is no place for hard work or determination," the students protested. "You seemed to give people an excuse for failure and sloppy performance by assuming that it is God's fault if we do not have the capabilities or opportunities to get ahead."

It is beyond human comprehension to understand why God uses some people in a prominent way while others, equally dedicated, serve in places of obscurity and live in poverty. My student critics were right. Our responsibility as Christians is to serve diligently, obediently, and to the best of our capabilities—whether or not we attain human success.

The Bible never implies that it is wrong to be rich, famous, or influential. But it is wrong to make these worldly marks of success our prime goal in life. It is wrong to manipulate or hurt others in our desire to get ahead. It is wrong to seek excuses to justify the lust for power and prestige. In contrast, the Christian who is successful seeks to encourage, help, and build up others. He or she is diligent in work, obedient to God, and willing to be used by Him wherever He leads, however He leads, and whether or not He permits us to appear successful.

This is an unpopular message, completely at odds with the values of our society. It goes against the teachings of most self-help books on success. Nevertheless, it is the basis of real and lasting success in God's eyes, whether or not we are wealthy, or acclaimed by the society in which we live.

18

HOW TO HANDLE
vacations

I'm not sure how it started—my love of traveling—but in my past I was bitten with a fascination for faraway places, and I've been on the go ever since. When the Sunday paper appears with its travel section, I read the articles with enthusiasm and linger over the advertisements. I think about trips that would be great to take, if only we had the time and money. I often dream about going to the places on my still-to-visit list.

I must admit, however, that traveling has taught me to be a little skeptical about some of those newspaper reports and advertisements. In spite of their color-saturated pictures and inviting descriptions, travel brochures rarely mention that there are times when the sun doesn't shine at Disneyland, when there's fog in the Alps, and when it's cold at the beach. People often get upset stomachs when they visit foreign countries. Sometimes they get seasick, even on those alluring cruises. The Queen isn't always greeting the crowds in London, and visitors don't always see the colorful national costumes or exotic animals that decorate the travel posters.

Don't misunderstand me! None of this keeps me from traveling, but even once-a-year vacationers discover that resorts, retreats, and recreational trips don't always come forth with the fun and problem-free relaxation that we expect. So many are the problems involved with handling vacations that psychologists even have a name for such stress. They call it the *vacation blues syndrome.*

At times it hits all of us, and it comes for a number of reasons. Consider, for example, the influence of:

• *An inability to relax.* Some people have trouble unwinding. Most of us know hard-driving achievers who take pride in never stopping and who hate to waste time. For such people there may be nothing worse than a week on a cruise ship or a few days isolated at a cottage in the mountains. When people can't relax, vacations can create the kinds of pressure that they are supposed to reduce.

• *Guilt.* Have you ever spent money on a vacation when there were bills unpaid? Have you taken a trip when a loved one had to remain at home? Have you ever gone fishing when you knew there were projects around the house that should get done? Have you found yourself charging souvenirs when you know, in your heart, that you can't afford what you are buying? All this can create guilt, which subtly gnaws away at the vacationer.

• *Pressure.* Sometimes we don't plan our vacations very well, we eat too much, we try to squeeze too much into two short weeks, or we fail to take enough money. All these are pressures that can leave us more tired at the end of our vacation than we were at the beginning.

• *Family closeness.* For many people one of the best things about vacations is visiting with relatives or traveling as a family. But for others such closeness can be devastating, especially when family members don't get along with each other very well.

• *Disappointment.* We usually expect a lot from our vacations, but sometimes those times away are not as exotic, rewarding, or pressure-free as our imaginations or travel brochures might lead us to expect. One travel association has estimated that three people out of every five are disappointed with the way their vacations turn out.

• *Change.* Somebody has defined the tourist as a person who travels to a place because it is different, and then com-

plains constantly because things are not the way they are at
home. Vacations, of course, take us away from our normal
routines, but sometimes they also tax our ability to adjust to
novelty and change. Different customs, foods, and routines,
sometimes accompanied with different languages, can all create tension and add to our fatigue.

Not long ago I was on an airplane reading one of those
airline magazines that are tucked in the seat pockets. One
fascinating article discussed jet-lag, the twentieth-century
phenomenon that is caused by crossing too many time zones
too quickly. The symptoms are far from fatal, but they can be
frustrating, especially during the first few days in another
part of the world. When I visited Tokyo for the first time, my
daughter and I went for a walk at 4 AM. because we couldn't
sleep, but later we had trouble staying awake through the
lunch hour. To make matters worse, I was scheduled to speak
at a meeting that began right after lunch—when it was sunny
and warm in the Orient, but the middle of the night at home.

For most of us these kinds of adjustments help to make
vacations challenging and even more fun. Traffic jams, flat
tires, strange lumpy beds, dull museums, booked tennis
courts, mosquitoes, rain, jet-lag, and even boring relatives can
all be taken in stride if we recognize that most vacations will
not be perfect. When we get back home even some of the
most frustrating parts of a trip can take on a humorous glow.

This gets us to some of the ways we can handle vacations and make them more relaxing and enjoyable.

First, ponder the importance of vacations. For some people this
is no hurdle. They believe in the importance of getting away
and they plan their vacations carefully, enthusiastically, and
well in advance.

There are others, however, who need to be reminded
that the Lord doesn't expect us to work all the time. After
creating the universe, God rested, and the Bible instructs us
to do the same (Gen. 2:2–3). The ancient Israelites and the
early Christians each rested every seven days and took other

regular periods of time away from their normal routines. Jesus relaxed in the home of Mary, Martha, and Lazarus; even in the midst of a busy ministry He pulled away from the crowds to pray (Mark 1:35), and sometimes to rest (John 4:6).

There have been times in my life when I have bordered on becoming a workaholic. I am not proud of this. Even when I've been caught up in the excitement of creative time-consuming projects, I have realized that constant work can have an adverse influence both on me and on others—especially on my family. It can also drag down the quality of my work. People who never take vacations, and boast about it, are not doing a favor to themselves or to others. They are pushing their bodies and minds in ways God never intended.

Second, plan realistically. Some people find it almost impossible to take vacations. Very demanding occupations, invalid family members, or a lack of funds can keep us at home even when we want or desperately need a break. At such times there can be value in a mini-vacation—perhaps only a couple of days or even a few hours away. If we think about it creatively, there often are ways to provide for the needs at home and still pull away briefly.

When it *is* possible to take a longer time away, try to plan a vacation that fits your personality, your interests, your pocketbook. If you dislike golf, don't go to a golfing area; if you enjoy golf, don't take a cruise. Sometimes all this is easier said than done. When family members have different tastes and interests, some compromise will be necessary. My children, for example, like to swim while I like to sit and read. Modern motels let us do both.

In all your planning, try to avoid unrealistic expectations, too much driving, or too many activities for the time you have available. If you are planning a sightseeing trip, allow rest time, even if it comes for a couple of days between the time when you return home and the day when you go back to work. In a time of gasoline shortages and financial pressures, try to plan vacations close to home and without large outlays of money. But remember the cardinal rule of vacation planning: You probably will need twice as much money and half as much luggage as you think you will need.

Third, allow yourself some "space." If you are visiting other people or traveling as a family, try to allow time to blow off steam periodically. This can keep tension down and prevent people from getting on each other's nerves. What parents have not discovered that a half-hour stop to let the kids run in a park can do wonders to keep peace in the back seat for the next hundred miles?

Fourth, be flexible. Some of the things that annoy us on vacations are not worth getting upset about—jet-lag, for example. It can be frustrating, but with a little rest and some planning we can recover quickly and go on to enjoy the vacation.

Fifth, make sure you have some time for growing. Vacations often become times for hurrying, but there is no opportunity for reflection and meditation. Surely a vacation should enable us to rethink our priorities, do some planning, reexamine our life styles, and get better acquainted with our traveling companions.

And what about spiritual growth? I know a lady who believes that if you haven't taken some of your vacation time to pray and ponder your relationship with God, then you haven't really made best use of your time away. Perhaps she's right. We *should* find spiritual rejuvenation on a vacation as well as physical relaxation.

Sixth, don't be surprised if you have a post-vacation letdown. It isn't easy to return to a mailbox filled with bills and then go back to work, especially if your vacation was a great success. Many people find, however, that the days following a vacation can be a time for taking up their routines with new vigor. Sometimes before the vacation you can plan some special projects or "fun activities" to be done after you return home.

This makes an easier transition back to your regular activities and gives you something to look forward to when your vacation ends.

As we get older most of us can learn to slow down at vacation time and to get the rest and spiritual rejuvenation that we need. Even I'm learning not to crowd too much into trips.

19

HOW TO HANDLE
holidays

I've got a friend who hates holidays! He doesn't like the Fourth of July, Labor Day, or Thanksgiving—and he especially dislikes Christmas.

"These are family times," he told me recently," and I don't have a family nearby with whom I can celebrate. I hate it when all the stores are closed. I feel lonely when everyone is partying and I am not. I get discouraged when the whole world seems to be in a happy holiday mood, but I feel depressed."

I can understand my friend because, to be honest, I feel somewhat the same way and so, it seems, do many others. Psychologists, sociologists, and a host of writers have tried to understand why people get "holiday blues." The explanations are fascinating. Holidays are difficult, it has been suggested, because of:

Busyness. Have you ever gone for a "restful vacation" and come home exhausted? Seasonal holidays are often like that. They become hectic periods of preparing, shopping, entertaining, and sometimes collapsing. When we are involved in frantic busyness, we often discover three by-products creeping into our lives: irritability, intolerance, and inefficiency. All this can make us prone to discouragement, even when everyone else seems to be celebrating joyfully.

Unfulfilled expectations. Holidays are times when we expect happiness, presents, a spiritual uplift, and good times with our friends (not necessarily in that order). But what if the anticipated joys do not come? What if everyone else seems to be having fun but we are not? What if Thanksgiving or Christmas dinner parties turn out to be boring flops? When this happens, our soaring anticipations of holiday fulfillment plummet into weighty let-downs.

Old memories. Sometimes holidays are depressing because they remind us of the "good old days" that no longer are here, and of happy times spent with people who no longer are present. But holidays can also stir up memories of past loneliness, disappointment, family conflict, and anxiety.

Consider, for example, the man whose father got drunk at the office party every Christmas. This created a lot of fear and tension in the family during the last days of December, and memories of those stressful times still remain many years later.

Loneliness. I once spent Christmas alone in Europe. All my friends were with their families, experiencing togetherness. My little student room was a lonely place, so I went for a walk. But the day was cold and dreary, the streets were deserted, and the shops were all closed. Somehow the holly wreaths and the store-front decorations didn't do anything to lift my spirits.

For many people, including some families, every holiday is like that. Alone and without friends or relatives with whom to celebrate, the hours drag on in a depressing mixture of loneliness, boredom, self-pity, and herculean attempts to forget that for many people this is a special day of happiness.

The list of causes could keep going. For some people holidays bring guilt because there is unhappiness at a time when we are supposed to be happy about our God-given blessings or about the Savior's birth. Others struggle with jealousies and family tensions when the relatives get together for parties. Many people, especially those who live in northern climates, feel "down" when they think of the long, bleak, cold, gray (and sometimes white), winter months that are ahead.

So what can be done to make the holidays more meaningful and less draining?

Some people seem to think that the best solution is to find ways to escape. They try to forget about the holidays, get busy with other things, or dull their thinking with alcohol. Such avoidance tactics never solve anything, although they may hide the pain for a while.

A similar suggestion is that we ignore the problems. According to a writer in *Time* magazine, people who criticize Christmas are morbid diagnosticians who like to dispense solemn warnings about the depressing hazards that lurk in traditional seasonal celebrations. Perhaps grim pictures of holiday misery *are* overdone at times. Certainly not everyone is depressed when it is "the season to be jolly." But the *Time* writer's conclusion that "joining in . . . is the best remedy for the holiday blues" is another way of saying, "If you get busy and ignore the problems they will go away." That is an insensitive and, for many people, an unrealistic suggestion. If you find holidays difficult, recognize that a lot of people feel the same. Then think of some realistic ways to handle the problems. You can, for example:

Take time to ponder the meaning of holidays. Have you ever wondered how the people who experienced the first Christmas must have coped? Elisabeth and Zacharias were elderly. Mary and Joseph were young. The shepherds were poor and uneducated. The wise men were wealthy scholars. They all experienced some pressure at the time of Christ's birth, but we never think of them as being frenzied, depressed, or overwhelmed by the Christmas events. These people kept their attention focused not on their circumstances, but on their sovereign God and on the eternal significance of these special days.

Many years after His birth in a manger, Jesus found

Himself surrounded by crowds of needy people all making demands on His time. He didn't get flustered and discouraged, as so many of us do at holiday times. Even in His busyness, Jesus quietly pulled away to spend time with His Father (see Mark 1:32–35). Perhaps He asked for strength, wisdom in establishing priorities, and a divine perspective on His life and activities. Such periods of meditation are difficult to schedule, especially in times of hectic holiday preparation, but they are essential if we are to keep these special days in perspective and prevent seasonal exhaustion and discouragement.

Unfortunately, our attention is often focused on the customs that surround Christmas instead of on the reality of Christ's birth. One solution to this problem is to stop trying to combine the two. Our culture, rather than Christianity, is often the source of holiday traditions. So, as Christians, we don't need to feel obligated to participate in all of them. Instead, we can create new, alternate ways of doing things that will better express the values we see in the biblical account of Christ's birth.

Reevaluate your expectations of the holidays. In many homes, the holiday table doesn't quite look like the advertisements in the homemaker's magazines, the tree is not as perfect as we might like, the cookies don't always get baked, or sometimes the cards are not sent on time. This isn't because people don't try. Most do! But we must recognize both that holiday plans do not always move smoothly and that things need not be perfectly organized in order to be enjoyable and meaningful.

Plan your preparations for the holidays. The time to begin holiday preparations is well in advance. We usually recognize this in January, but perhaps this year we can do something about it in November. Decide what you must do, what you would like to do if time permits, and how you will schedule your time. Try to be realistic and not bound by the expectations of other people or by your own standards of perfection.

Recognize the strain of holidays. Holidays are golden opportunities for reaching out to others, especially to those who find these to be difficult times of the year. Even if you enjoy holidays, remember those who are less happy and try to include them in your plans and celebrations.

Do you remember the friend I mentioned who hates holidays? He and his wife are coming to our home for Christmas this year, and there undoubtedly will be others like them at our table. This isn't completely for the benefit of our guests. When we reach out to help others, we discover that it is not only a lot easier for us to handle the holidays, it's also more fun!

20

HOW TO HANDLE
aging

When we look back over our lives, most of us can point to events that were turning points—periods of crisis, sudden change, adventure, or reflection. These events altered the direction of our pilgrimages here on earth.

For me, one such turning point was a visit to Switzerland almost a decade ago. I had become interested in the writings of a Swiss counselor named Paul Tournier, and I went to Geneva to study his work. For almost a year, as I did my research, our whole family absorbed the beauty and richness of the Swiss culture. We lived in Cologny, a town on the outskirts of Geneva, where our little apartment seemed to be far from the imposing residences of diplomats and other important foreigners who reside in that international city. Many of our neighbors were Christians, brothers and sisters with whom we felt a bond of fellowship even though our use of the French language was far from fluent.

One of our neighbors was a vivacious lady whom I'll call Madame Laubry. Middle-aged, married, and the mother of three teen-age children, she was a dynamic Christian although her life had not been easy. A native of eastern Europe, she, with her family, had fled from Nazi oppression during the 1940s. Her postwar years had been darkened by the demands of a physically handicapped child who required almost constant care and attention.

One day Madame Laubry and I were discussing the issue

of aging. "One thing I know for sure," my middle-aged Swiss neighbor proclaimed with assurance, "I like being the age I am now. I do not long to be younger, and I'm not waiting to grow older. I have learned to enjoy the age I am at present."

A similar perspective emerged during some of my visits with Dr. Tournier. Unlike Madame Laubry, Tournier was in his seventies when I first met him. He had even written a book about growing old. The years had taken their toll, but the old doctor was alert, positive in attitude, and gracious in all his actions. He remains so today.

The process of growing old begins at the moment of conception, but few of us think much about aging until we are in our forties or fifties. Ours is a culture that values youth, and the arrival of middle-age sometimes brings the stunning realization that we no longer have the physical appearance and vigor that our society prizes. Our athletic potential is gone. Our early vocational direction has been set. In most cases our marriages have been launched, and some have crumbled. Our youthful dreams of fame and success may have given way to lives that are boring, meaningless, routine, problem-plagued, debt-infested, or wildly hectic. Some people try to break out of the middle-age mold. They may dress and talk like teenagers, break up their marriages, or abruptly change careers. Others become self-critical, angry, rebellious, or confused. Only a few can hide temporarily from the realities of middle-age and from personal self-examination which most of us experience as we move into the afternoon of life. Our teen-age and adult children remind us that we are no longer the younger generation. Our aging parents force us to recognize that we too may be weak, financially dependent, physically unattractive, or even senile in the not-too-distant future.

Aging, however, can be a positive growing experience. I learned that from my Swiss neighbors—Madame Laubry who likes being middle-aged and Dr. Tournier who is now in his eighties. Both have restrictions on their freedom, bodies that are wearing out, and opportunities that are gone forever. But both have a positive outlook on life and the realization that for the devoted follower of Jesus Christ, the best part of living is still ahead.

Have you noticed that some old people are bitter, cynical, and complaining, while others are sweet, loving, and compassionate even in the midst of family problems, financial pressures, and declining health? How did these differences occur? I suspect that complaining older people griped and scowled a lot when they were middle-aged or younger. In contrast, gracious, pleasant old people learned to be loving and understanding many years earlier.

There are numerous influences that affect our values and shape our thinking. The people with whom we associate, the books and magazines we read, the television programs we watch, the music to which we listen, the thoughts with which we fill our minds—all these mold our attitudes toward life as we grow older. In the end, writes Phillip Keller, we are the sum total of our earlier choices. For young people and for those who are middle-aged (that means those of us who remember Harry Truman, Collier's magazine, Fibber McGee's closet, Baby Snooks, and a song called "Jeepers Creepers"), now is the time to make choices that will prepare us for the later years. Our preparations can involve several activities.

First, we can *accept* our age. It's helpful to pause periodically and ponder the advantages of being and growing older. Of course there are problems and challenges—this is true for people at every period in life—but as we grow older there is a sense of being settled, of having found one's place in society, and of being freed from the demands of raising small children. Most of us have not succeeded in everything, as we once hoped. But in contrast to young people, middle-aged and older people often have greater wisdom, more opportunity to travel, some financial security, and increased opportunities to serve others in our communities and churches. A bygone generation used to say, "Life begins at forty." There may be some truth in that old adage. Like Madame Laubry, perhaps we should determine to accept our middle-age and attempt to live this period of life to the fullest.

There's also value in *self-examination* and realistic planning for the future. Tournier once wrote that the passage from adulthood to old age is not a step backwards. It can be an advance into a time of new fulfillment and greater breadth of interest and service. But the transition begins long before retirement. It comes when we are in our fifties, or even in our forties. It comes as we ponder questions such as:

• How will I spend the rest of my life?

• Should I make changes in my attitudes, priorities, and values?

• Are there responsible changes that I should make in my vocation, marriage, or lifestyle?

• If so, how can I change?

• What will I do and how will I live after retirement?

• What can I do now that will help me experience a meaningful old age?

When these issues are considered and discussed earlier in life, the transition to old age is eased and sometimes even anticipated with pleasure.

Another way to handle aging is so simple that it is easily overlooked: *Take care of your body.* Get into the practice of regular exercise and consistent rest. Work to keep down your weight, get periodic physical checkups, and try to avoid the pollutants that so often speed the process of aging. And in caring for the body, don't forget your mind. Take some time to expand your interests, to read, to learn about things that are new. Try some creative hobbies, take a night course, and get involved in your church or community. If you are too involved already, ponder which of your activities might be eliminated so there is more time for relaxation, contemplation, and new challenges.

In all this remember the importance of *giving.* Loneliness rarely comes to people who are interested in others, caring, and sincere in their efforts to help. The Bible repeatedly states the importance of reaching out to those in need. Of course the recipient of such giving is often benefited, but the one who gives is helped even more.

So far our discussion of aging has focused on the preretirement years. But how do we handle aging after we reach retirement? In the United States alone, the over-65 population increases at a rate of over 1,600 every day. For some this is a time of continued health and meaningful activity, but for others the later years are characterized by isolation, uncertainty, illness, loneliness, financial pressure, and discouragement. This was expressed succinctly by a lady whom I met recently on the West Coast. "I'm old," she said, with tears in her eyes, "and I don't like it!"

Although our Western society doesn't always respect old age, it is good to remember that God does. The Bible assures us of divine care for the aged, and we know that God is pleased when younger people provide for those who are older (1 Tim. 5:4). In Psalm 27, David wrote that he could take courage and "wait for the Lord" because he knew that God does not forsake us, even when others have left. For the believer in Jesus Christ, the best is yet to be. We can prepare to meet the Lord face to face and spend eternity with him.

In the meantime, as the years pass, we all become more limited in our activities and abilities. Nevertheless, with God's help we each can learn to accept where we are in life, realistically plan for the future (including a future of life after death), take care of our bodies and minds as best we can, and ponder how we can reach out in giving to others—even if our resources are limited and travel away from home is difficult.

My Swiss friend Tournier has faced some of these decisions. When his wife died several years ago, he felt that a part of him had been torn away. His health did not permit active work in his vocation, and life could have ended in despair and loneliness. But Tournier has continued to reach out—graciously receiving visitors, corresponding with people in need, and to the best of his ability serving God in old age.

A recent report estimated that at least one-fifth of our population suffers from something called "gerontophobia"—the fear of growing old. We can learn to overcome such fears. Like my Swiss friends, we can recognize that while each period of life holds difficulties, each can be a period of fulfillment. The time to start handling the challenges of aging is now. We will never be any younger!

21

HOW TO HANDLE
singleness

The crashing thunder was so loud that it seemed to shake the whole house. Without thinking, I leaped out of bed and stumbled to close the window, which already was alive with the rapid-fire sounds of pounding raindrops and hail. I glanced at the clock (4:12 A.M.), and only then did I notice that my wife was not in bed.

"She's probably gone to close the other windows or to reassure one of the kids," I reasoned, but it soon became apparent that no windows were open, and that our children were both sleeping soundly in spite of the clamor.

Then I found her. My wife was sitting on the edge of the tub in our windowless bathroom, trying to calm our nervous German Shepherd, who is big and brave in all circumstances—except storms. It probably would not have been good for me to laugh (at least until morning), but the situation did seem humorous. Instead of sleeping, like everyone else in the house, we were trying to convince a dog that in spite of the storm, everything would soon be all right.

Later in the day when my mind was more awake, I began to ponder the difficulty of getting that dog to think differently. How good it would be if the animal could understand and deliberately change its thinking about thunder and lightning. But animals, even intelligent animals, are limited in their reasoning ability, and sometimes even people have attitudes and ideas that resist change. In difficult circumstances we all tend to slip into thinking that is self-defeating, self-condemning, and unchanging.

Consider singleness, for example. Like married people, single adults struggle at times with discouragement, financial pressures, health problems, interpersonal conflicts, and spiritual doubt. But never-married and formerly married people also grapple with issues that are common among singles: Where do I fit into this society where most adults walk in pairs? How do I find companionship and avoid loneliness? What do I do with my God-given sex drives? These are difficult questions to answer, but perhaps the place to start is with our thinking. Changing our mind-set is a first step to handling the challenges of singleness.

The Misfit Mentality characterizes many unmarried adults. This is a way of thinking which assumes that "since most people are married, and I am single, then I must be a misfit, out of step with the majority in our society." Even though almost 50 million American adults are unmarried, it is easy for singles to conclude that they are alone, unacceptable, and perhaps unwanted.

Such tragic thinking sometimes is stimulated by well-meaning but insensitive friends, parents, and others who conclude in error that all single people must be afraid of intimacy, threatened by sex, unwilling to leave home, or even homosexual. At times unmarried seminary graduates cannot get pastorates because of their singleness, and it often is assumed that adults are not really mature and responsible until they "settle down" in marriage. As a result, singles often have trouble getting a mortgage, a credit rating, or a decent seat in restaurants. Even songs and books contribute to the misfit image. "You're nobody 'til somebody loves you" was once a popular ballad which didn't do much to build the single person's self confidence. Almost as bad are book titles like "Single and Satisfied" or "Single and Human."

Even before I got married (at the ripe old age of twenty-nine), I had begun to sense that some people harbor a prejudice against single adults. Many more, apparently, don't know how to relate to single people and wonder if unmarried friends should ever be invited to family gatherings or to dinner parties where most of the guests are married. (The answer is "yes.")

Single and married people must all work to resist the misfit mentality. Remember that Jesus and Paul were unmarried, and the Bible even cites what is in at least one sense the superiority of the single life (I Cor. 7:8, 32–35). All human beings are created in the image of God. When we fell into sin, God loved us so much that He sent His Son to die for our sins. He never forces us to become Christians, but those who commit their lives to Him become new, "born-again" creatures who are God's adopted children with abundant life on earth and the promise of eternal life in heaven after death. None of this depends on our marital status. God loves us all equally and does not accept the misfit mentality. We, too, must decide to reject this harmful idea that single people are all misfits.

The Maintenance Mentality assumes that singles should maintain their present way of living until marriage comes along to make life better and to give life a purpose. People who think this way live in the future, often avoiding important decisions or careful life planning because of the possibility that a marriage might "change everything." Life thus becomes a holding pattern, characterized by waiting, inactivity, drifting, floundering, and sometimes boredom. Most tragic is the fact that such thinking frequently characterizes younger people who are at the most alert, energetic, and capable period in life.

When I graduated from college, each of us had our portrait in the university yearbook, accompanied by a list of our extracurricular activities and a quotation from some famous person. I chose the words of a cartoonist named Walt Kelly who wrote: "Too soon we breast the tape, and too late we realize that the fun lay in the running."

There is nothing wrong with anticipating the possibility of marriage. But to live in the future is as self-defeating as the thinking of those older people who live with their minds always dwelling on the good old days of the past. In reality, we live in the present, and, whether single or married, we must cultivate interests, develop a personality, take responsibility, learn about interpersonal relationships, find a purpose for living, and serve both Christ and others unselfishly—now. To squelch our careers, friendships, financial planning, and spiritual development while we wait for a hoped-for marriage is to miss the joy of living and to miss the fun that comes with running through life. A maintenance mentality can also make individuals dull and less desirable as marriage partners.

The Me Mentality which permeates our whole society assumes that "I am the center of my universe. My major purposes in life are to meet my own needs, to solve my own problems, and to provide for my personal comfort and well-being. Self-denial, self-discipline, or self-sacrifice have little place in my life. Self-fulfillment, self-satisfaction, and self-realization are far more important."

Recently I had lunch with the editor of a large and growing magazine for singles. "We get dozens of articles telling readers how to help themselves," he reported, "but to this point nobody has submitted even one article suggesting that we should consider ways of reaching out to help others."

It is easy for any of us to get wound up in our own problems. Loneliness, discouragement, confusion about the present, concern about the future, and a variety of other issues can consume vast amounts of time and energy. Personal tensions also can pull us into a confining net of self-centered introspection where we are bound by our own concerns and unable to see the needs of others.

Such me-centered thinking causes us to miss one of the most rewarding aspects of human existence—the fulfillment that comes from helping and serving others. It is even true that sometimes the best way to help ourselves is to help others. The members of Alcoholics Anonymous discovered this many years ago, and generations of people have proved it throughout history.

It is never wise to ignore our stresses and personal needs (problems that are pushed out of mind have a way of popping up repeatedly until they are resolved), but thoughts about ourselves must be balanced with a sincere interest in others coupled with practical acts of compassion and care. In the Bible, this is the theme of the book of James, and the idea of helping one another permeates the entire writings of the apostle Paul.

The Mad Mentality involves anger and hostility. I know a number of people, single and married, who appear to be basically angry. They are resentful, self-righteous in their thinking, and caught in what one person has called the "hostility trap." Some singles are mad at themselves, at others, and even at God because of their singleness. The Bible and modern psychology agree that such bitterness can lead to all kinds of trouble (Heb. 12:15), including physical illness, conflicts with others, and inner discouragement.

We don't deal with anger by pretending that it doesn't exist. We admit it to ourselves, confess it to God, discuss it with one or two others, and attempt to find ways in which we can reduce it. Try to determine what causes your anger, and then think of practical ways in which you can deal with these causes. In all this, don't forget to look for the bright side of life. By concentrating on things that are wrong or unjust, we stimulate anger, and this blinds us to things that are right, just, pure, and worthwhile. Each of us can decide individually whether or not we will wallow in the misery of a mad mentality or change our thinking to something more positive.

The Maturing Mentality is more healthy. Have you ever noticed how often the Bible refers to the mind? We are instructed to have a mind like Christ, to be like-minded with other believers, and to let our minds dwell on thoughts that are positive and uplifting. Elsewhere we are urged to "renew" the mind so that our thinking is more mature and in accordance with the will of God.

According to Romans 12, the person with a maturing mind:

• takes care of the body, keeping it pure and in good shape so that our thinking is not clouded by physical distractions;

• resists conforming to society's values (which surely includes misfit, maintenance, me-first, and mad ways of thinking);

• seeks to know and do the will of God;

• is humble, not conceited, and able to accept the fact that God has made us each unique with individual gifts, responsibilities, and, I suspect, marital status opportunities;

• is concerned about others, characterized by an attitude of love and concern which enables us to rejoice with those who rejoice and to weep with those who weep;

• is diligent and enthusiastic in serving the Lord; and

• is determined to get along with others.

The way we think can often determine how we will handle the stresses of life—including the pressures of being single. We can go through life with an "isn't it awful" attitude, or we can develop maturing minds which enable us to cope effectively with the tensions of life.

I think I'll try to remember this next time we have a storm. That dog of ours still hates thunder and seems to need human companionship, especially when it rains in the middle of the night. On such occasions there is plenty of time for me to ponder my own type of thinking. Perhaps I'll even think of a way to get the kids to handle the dog's anxieties next time we have a storm.

22

HOW TO HANDLE
burnout

Recently I received a letter from a friend in London who had an unusual request. After commenting about a book I had written, she asked if there was some way it could be "translated from American into English." Her request started me thinking about the ways in which words take on new meanings in our language.

Consider, for example, "cool chick," a term that has nothing to do with cold chicken. "Turning on," "far out," "fox," "gay,"—these are among the words that have accepted meanings other than those given in the dictionary. Another word is "burnout." As used in psychological circles, this word has no reference to defective light bulbs, but it does describe an experience that is common in those of us who spend a lot of time in contact with other people.

Burnout refers to a feeling of physical and emotional exhaustion which comes after we have had prolonged involvement with people and work situations that demand our time, energy, and strength. Several years ago the term "burnout" was used to describe counselors and other professional people helpers who had become tense, discouraged, and overwhelmed by the demands of working intensively and for hours with people in need. More recently, it has become clear that counselors are not the only people who burn out. Policemen, physicians, social workers, business executives, nurses, teachers, lawyers, sales people, pastors, missionaries, parachurch workers, and probably a great many parents are among those who experience periodic burnout, especially in times of extra pressure such as Christmas. The questionnaire that accompanies this chapter lists some of the characteristics of burnout. You might want to complete this test before reading further.

It isn't easy to interact intensively and continually with people who are hurting, under pressure, or inclined to demand a lot from us. Needy people, including the people we live with and work with, demand a lot of our time, energy,

---

ARE YOU BURNED OUT?

For each statement, circle whether this is *rarely* true (R) in your life, *sometimes* true (S), or *usually* true (U).

R	S	U	
0	1	2	I feel exhausted and run down.
0	1	2	I am irritable.
0	1	2	I get frustrated easily.
0	1	2	I feel helpless.
0	1	2	I have trouble sleeping.
0	1	2	I am discouraged.
0	1	2	I tend to be critical of others.
0	1	2	I tend to be critical of myself.
0	1	2	I want to get away from people.
0	1	2	I would like to change my job.
0	1	2	I feel spiritually dull.
0	1	2	I think that my job is stressful.
0	1	2	I feel under constant pressure.
0	1	2	I have difficulty being with troubled people.
0	1	2	I am impatient.
0	1	2	I lack enthusiasm.

If you scored in the range of 16–32 points, you may be a victim of burnout.

and concentration, and sometimes they can give little in return. When these people suffer we often feel sad. When they criticize we feel hurt. And it can be distressing to watch as others fall into sin, lose their health, make unwise choices, or grapple with difficult decisions. Sometimes we blame ourselves because we have been unable to help, and this can lead to guilt and self-criticism.

The most intensive study of burnout ever reported was completed recently at the University of California in Berkeley. Researchers interviewed several hundred people, all of whom were having trouble coping with emotional stress that comes from intimate involvement with troubled human beings. The research discovered that there are several signs which indicate that burnout is developing.

As burnout approaches, *we detach ourselves from other people.* Sometimes this involves staying home, avoiding social situations, and spending less time with others. We can also become aloof, cynical, and less involved emotionally. In a study of burned out policemen, researchers discovered a tendency for these men to be tough, noncommunicative, and distant, even at home. Such withdrawal from others lets us protect ourselves and reduce pressures.

Of course it isn't always possible to withdraw from demanding children, tense work situations, or people who are needy. Very often we keep pushing ourselves until *we begin to run down physically.* Headaches, a greater vulnerability to disease, fatigue, or a loss of physical energy can all indicate that something is wrong.

In addition, *we are influenced psychologically.* Discouragement, low morale, impatience, self-condemnation, forgetfulness, a hypercritical attitude, inefficiency, and a "what's the use" attitude can all slip into our thinking. It is hard to be a good mother or father if you are burned out. It is not easy to be an effective pastor if you feel overwhelmed by people. And when burnout occurs at work or school, there often is low morale, job dissatisfaction, conflict between workers, frequent absenteeism, impaired performance, and lowered productivity. Some people try to dull all this with alcohol or

some other drug, but this solves nothing. Some try to overcome the problem by working harder, but this only increases
the frustration. Many "take it out" on their families and
become harder to live with at home. Then there are those
who quit their jobs, move away from needy people, or per-
form so poorly that they get fired.

But we need not quit. Think about Jesus, for example.
Although He was surrounded by people much of the time,
many of whom were needy and demanding, Jesus never
burned out. Modern researchers have discovered how we can
handle burnout, but their conclusions are remarkably similar
to the ways in which Jesus lived His life.

To prevent burnout we need time alone. There were periods in
His life when Jesus pulled away from the crowds so that He
could interact with the disciples, relax in the home of Mary
and Martha, or be by Himself in prayer and meditation.
Research has shown that such periods of withdrawal are
essential if we are to prevent burnout. Short rest periods and
times for coffee may be helpful, but periodically we need
longer breaks for at least a few days away from demanding
kids, sick relatives, clinging parishioners, or the needy people
with whom we work.

Recently on a trip to the West Coast I discovered that
my luggage had not been placed on the plane when I left
Chicago. Many of my fellow travelers had made a similar
discovery, and some were less than gracious as they crowded
into the "Lost Baggage" office. When I got to the counter I
asked the lady in charge how she was able to deal with so
many frustrated and angry people. "I can handle it for eight
hours," she replied, "but if I don't pull away by myself for a
while after work, I'm pretty hard to live with." Sometimes it
is best for everyone involved if we withdraw periodically to
find refreshment and renewal.

To prevent burnout we need shared responsibilities. Even Jesus,
who is all-powerful and could have done everything without
help, trained His followers and encouraged them to work

together in the task of making disciples. Nothing hastens burnout like the belief that there is no one else to help. Professional counselors have found that burnout is less likely and work is more efficient when the professionals can get together to discuss problems, to get advice, and to help each other. Such sharing can be helpful for all of us.

In a sense, this contradicts the North American philosophy of rugged individualism. We often think that it is a sign of strength and competence when we can handle a job alone. We are reluctant to seek help and sometimes even less willing to accept assistance. Some of us conclude, at times correctly, that others can't do a job as well as we can, and there may be feelings of guilt in letting others try to help.

Recently my wife and I were discussing the challenges of child rearing with some other parents. "It's hard for us to get away as a couple," one lady said. "We don't have any relatives nearby, and it is expensive to hire full-time baby sitters." Almost immediately someone responded that parents can and should help one another by sharing child care responsibilities so each couple can retreat periodically. Is there someone who can relieve some of your load for a while? Can you help someone else? Sharing responsibilities can reduce the risk of burnout.

To prevent burnout we need body support. Each of us needs close contact with people who can give encouragement and a different perspective, especially when we are under pressure. Do you remember Jesus in the Garden of Gethsemane? He found genuine comfort in praying, but He also wanted the disciples to be awake and near Him as He approached the hour of crucifixion.

In the New Testament Epistles the church is described as a body of believers who are to accept, encourage, and care for one another. There is no such thing as "go it alone" Christian growth, and neither can there be a "do it yourself" prevention for burnout. If you are not yet burned out, seek and maintain contacts with supportive Christian friends whom you enjoy and who can give meaningful human contact.

But what if you feel that all this is too late? What if burnout is a present reality for you rather than a remote possibility? What if you circled mostly two's on the questionnaire that accompanies this article?

To recognize the presence of burnout is a first step in coping. To accept the fact that you are presently overwhelmed by people or circumstances is a positive move toward improvement. It may be that you feel uncomfortable talking about this with other people, but try to find at least one person who can be encouraging, able to listen, and willing to help you get a better perspective on your life pressures. Don't be afraid to seek the assistance of a pastor or other Christian counselor who can help you cope with stress. Ask yourself, "How can I pull away? With whom can I share some of my responsibilities? Is it possible that some things can be left undone until later?"

Remember too that God has promised to give us peace and direction. Jesus is with us always, whether or not we realize this. A recognition of this divine presence can be a great source of help and support in time of need.

Burnout is a common experience among people whose jobs and families require them to give constantly and completely to other people in need. If burnout doesn't influence you, it probably is affecting someone that you know. Burnout can be prevented and handled, however, if we are aware of its influence and willing to tackle it courageously.

In doing this we might even be able to eliminate burnout, and then we wouldn't have to use the word. My British friend would like that. It would make it easier for her to translate this chapter into English!

23

HOW TO HANDLE
the future

I have some mixed feelings about Alvin Toffler!

Maybe you don't recognize the name, but he once wrote a best-selling book titled *Future Shock*. It was clearly written, fascinating, and so persuasive that it jolted a whole generation of people. The book convinced many readers that things in this world are changing a lot faster than we thought, or than we might like.

It's bad enough to be coping with rising prices, teenage kids, grey hairs, wrinkles, and brown spots—like my grandfather used to have on his hands. But Toffler and other experts on the future say we haven't seen anything yet! The pace of life is speeding up (I've been noticing that), and there seem to be mind-boggling changes in our standards of living, views of right and wrong, approaches to education and business, family commitments, developments in science or technology, and even in our opinions of sacred things like patriotism, religion, and motherhood.

There are radical changes taking place in transportation, economics, pollution control, energy resources, electronics, the media, and food production, to name a few. If you've thought about doing some reading in an effort to keep up, "forget it!" Over one thousand new books are published *every day,* and if you like reading scientific papers, every year 60 million pages of technical articles appear. Even speed readers can't keep up with that!

If all this change seems overwhelming, then join the crowd. This feeling of confusion and disorientation is what we mean by future shock. I suppose we should thank Toffler for telling us about it, but sometimes I wish we hadn't been informed so dramatically. If we can't keep up with the pace of life now, what's going to happen as things change even faster in the future?

It's easy to understand why some people prefer to ignore all this, hoping perhaps that the changes can be overlooked. Others give up in despair or disgust, and more than a few brave souls go running through life in a never-ending, vain attempt to "keep up with what's going on."

But there are better ways to handle the future. Although it might be good for us to think positively about what we *should* do to face our troubles, in this final chapter it could be even more helpful to mention some things that we *should not* do as we move toward the twenty-first century.

Don't take problems too seriously. This is a book about the tensions and struggles of life, and repeatedly you have been urged to face problems honestly when they arise. It is possible, however, to take ourselves and our problems too seriously?

Sometimes I wish that I was not a psychologist. People in my profession have a tendency to be overly introspective, and sometimes, it seems, we explore issues with so much detail that we get bogged down in superanalysis.

I'm not changing my mind now and suggesting that you overlook problems, but I am proposing that we all need to balance our introspection with an appreciation of the good things in life. We relieve a lot of tension when we learn to laugh at ourselves, to enjoy people, and to put our troubles aside temporarily. It can be pleasurable and relaxing to think about things that (to use the Bible's words) are true, honorable, right, pure, lovely, good, excellent, and praiseworthy (Phil. 4:8). According to the Old Testament, there is "an appointed time for everything. . . . A time to weep, and a time to laugh; a time to mourn, and time to dance" (Eccles. 3:1, 4).

When we forget this need to laugh or dance, we can become stuffy, judgmental, self-centered, and sometimes inflated with a belief in our own importance. At times, therefore, our weeping and mourning must be put aside while we laugh and express our joy.

Don't let things get out of perspective. Most of us have noticed how fear and imagination sometimes cause worry about things that never happen. Any one of us can get so worried about the country, the economy, the shortage of natural resources, or—what is more likely—we can get so concerned about our jobs, marriages, or children, that we can't move. Sometimes, by worrying and doing little else, we even permit or bring about the things that worry us most. Have you ever met people who fret so much about not being liked that they drive their friends away? That is a way of increasing problems by getting them out of perspective.

We must remember that the future, like the present, is in God's hands. He who created the world is now holding it all together (Col. 1:16–17), and He tells us not to worry about tomorrow (Matt. 6:34), regardless of how quickly things might change.

Jesus didn't tell us to ignore the future, however. We cannot be sure what is ahead in our lifetimes, and we aren't able to control the future completely. Nevertheless, it is wise to give thought to where we are going (Prov. 14:15). We should try to keep aware of what is going on around us, and trust that God will use us to influence the future direction of our families, communities, and professions.

In all of the earth's history, there probably has been no time as exciting as the age in which we live. We can react with despair and worry, or we can accept all this change as being permitted by a God who also will help us adapt. We don't adapt very well when we ignore changes or let them overwhelm us. That is getting things out of perspective, and it brings us to a third suggestion about the future.

Don't ignore or deny problems. If you've read some of the preceding chapters, you may have noticed that one conclusion has come up again and again: the first step in solving any problem is to admit that it exists.

It isn't always easy to admit that problems exist. Even with all its emphasis on openness, honesty, sharing, and counseling, ours is a society that admires rugged independence and the ability of people to overcome their own difficulties. We sometimes feel like failures if our personal struggles don't go away, but the sooner we face these issues, the sooner we start to find solutions.

Don't overlook the importance of other people. Shortly after the creation, God told Adam that he needed a "helper," since it is not good for us to be alone. Shortly after that helper arrived, there was conflict, and the scene was set for interpersonal tensions which have characterized history ever since. We humans have always had trouble getting along with each other, but we have also seen how much we can help one another.

During my lifetime, I have taken several trips to the Orient. With each trip, I like it better, especially the people. They are hospitable and gracious, but I also have noticed that many attach great importance to "saving face." Some seem reluctant to admit mistakes, to acknowledge that there are problems which haven't been solved, or to ask for help. At first I concluded that this was "typically Oriental," but I'm beginning to think it's "typically Western" as well. To ask for help is to admit that we haven't been able to solve our own problems, and that's threatening.

Once we admit to ourselves that a problem exists, it is important to talk with God about it, and then it can be helpful to tell somebody else. From the beginning of human history, God apparently intended that we humans would be givers and receivers of help. We must not forget this as we work to handle present and future problems.

There are many times in life when each of us could

benefit from some counseling. Most often, we get this from our friends or relatives, but when they can't help it may be wise to seek the aid of a professional counselor. If such a suggestion makes you feel uncomfortable, then take courage in the fact that this is a common reaction. Even to admit your reluctance can be a step toward recovery.

Stated simply, there is a need for professional help when: You or somebody in your family is emotionally distressed and having trouble coping with the common responsibilities of life; there is a lack of efficient communication in the family; and/or your repeated efforts seem unable to resolve these difficulties. At such times you need a negotiator who can help you see things more clearly and learn how to change.

Most personal problems involve more than the person who is hurting. Problems influence entire families, and sometimes the whole family needs counseling. For example, if somebody in your family is depressed, alcoholic, extremely anxious, or struggling with some other problem, it is of no help for you to say "snap out of it—you shouldn't feel like you do." If you or somebody in the family *believes* that a problem exists, it *does* exist, and it affects everyone in the family including those who are convinced that nothing is wrong.

But even when you accept the need for counseling, it isn't easy to pick up the phone and call a professional counselor. A big problem is deciding whom to call. Those "counselors" listed in the yellow pages of your telephone directory probably will include both those who are capable and some who are not very competent. Before calling, therefore, do some checking. Try to locate the names of counselors who are known to have a good reputation and who are competently trained. If you can, find out about the personalities of local counselors and about their attitudes to your faith. It isn't always necessary to find a counselor who believes exactly like you do, but it is best if you can talk with someone who respects your religion and doesn't try to undermine your moral standards.

As you well know, it isn't easy to get such information, but a good place to start is with your pastor or physician. These people are likely to know the counselors in your area. Friends can also make recommendations.

When you get to the counselor, don't hesitate to ask polite questions about fees, the counselor's training, his or her approach, the length of time involved, or any other issues of concern. Any counselor who is competent won't be threatened or put off by such inquiries. Remember, too, that you are under no obligation. If necessary, visit more than one counselor until you find the best person available.

Then be as cooperative as possible. A lot of counseling success or failure depends on your willingness to learn and to take responsibility for expressing feelings and concerns honestly, looking at things in a new light, and changing behavior.

Don't rely on a dead religion. I'm not sure if it's true, but a friend once told me about the visit of a pastor who went to the home of a church family. In an attempt to impress this visitor, the father called one of the children to the living room.

"Johnny," the man requested, "while the pastor is here, please go to the bedroom and get that old book that our family loves so much and that your mother and I read together so often."

With enthusiasm, the boy ran off to the bedroom and returned happily clutching the Sears catalog!

Sometimes, religion becomes something put on to impress others, but it doesn't really permeate our lives. We go to church on Sunday, read the Bible on rare occasions, and act as if God is far away—available to be summoned if needed but otherwise not of much importance.

The Bible calls this dead religion (James 1:26). It is worthless because it involves words only. It doesn't really change our lives, and like a rusty lawn mower that hasn't been used for years, it doesn't work very well when needed—in times of crisis and change.

The Christian faith involves *belief* in Jesus Christ and

obedience to His lordship. Faith without obedience is dead, but faith that involves obedience is lively and exciting. When your faith grows cold, you don't thaw out by trying to muster up more faith. You *act* as if you had an exciting religion, and you soon discover that obedience strengthens your beliefs.

Have you ever heard someone say, "I don't feel love for my husband any more"? The way to restore such love is not by trying to stir up feelings. Engage in loving actions and loving feelings are likely to follow.

That's a good conclusion to keep in mind as we cope with change and try to face the future shock which Toffler has described so vividly. We are not alone in this old world. We have one another, and we have a God who is in control of the universe and who cares even when we ignore Him. He can help us to obey Him and to put our confidence in His son Jesus Christ. To yield to Him in humble submission, the Bible tells us (John 10:10; 3:16), is to bring an abundant life on earth now and eternal life in heaven. That's where the change and future shock of this world will concern us no longer.

CHRISTIAN HERALD ASSOCIATION AND ITS MINISTRIES

CHRISTIAN HERALD ASSOCIATION, founded in 1878, publishes The Christian Herald Magazine, one of the leading interdenominational religious monthlies in America. Through its wide circulation, it brings inspiring articles and the latest news of religious developments to many families. From the magazine's pages came the initiative for CHRISTIAN HERALD CHILDREN'S HOME and THE BOWERY MISSION, two individually supported not-for-profit corporations.

CHRISTIAN HERALD CHILDREN'S HOME, established in 1894, is the name for a unique and dynamic ministry to disadvantaged children, offering hope and opportunities which would not otherwise be available for reasons of poverty and neglect. The goal is to develop each child's potential and to demonstrate Christian compassion and understanding to children in need.

Mont Lawn is a permanent camp located in Bushkill, Pennsylvania. It is the focal point of a ministry which provides a healthful "vacation with a purpose" to children who without it would be confined to the streets of the city. Up to 1000 children between the ages of 7 and 11 come to Mont Lawn each year.

Christian Herald Children's Home maintains year-round contact with children by means of an *In-City Youth Ministry*. Central to its philosophy is the belief that only through sustained relationships and demonstrated concern can individual lives be truly enriched. Special emphasis is on individual guidance, spiritual and family counseling and tutoring. This follow-up ministry to inner-city children culminates for many in financial assistance toward higher education and career counseling.

THE BOWERY MISSION, located at 227 Bowery, New York City, has since 1879 been reaching out to the lost men on the Bowery, offering them what could be their last chance to rebuild their lives. Every man is fed, clothed and ministered to. Countless numbers have entered the 90-day residential rehabilitation program at the Bowery Mission. A concentrated ministry of counseling, medical care, nutrition therapy, Bible study and Gospel services awakens a man to spiritual renewal within himself.

These ministries are supported solely by the voluntary contributions of individuals and by legacies and bequests. Contributions are tax deductible. Checks should be made out either to CHRISTIAN HERALD CHILDREN'S HOME or to THE BOWERY MISSION.

Administrative Office: 40 Overlook Drive, Chappaqua, New York 10514
Telephone: (914) 769-9000